LOOK AND REMEMBER
History Book I I

TUDORS AND STUARTS

Contents

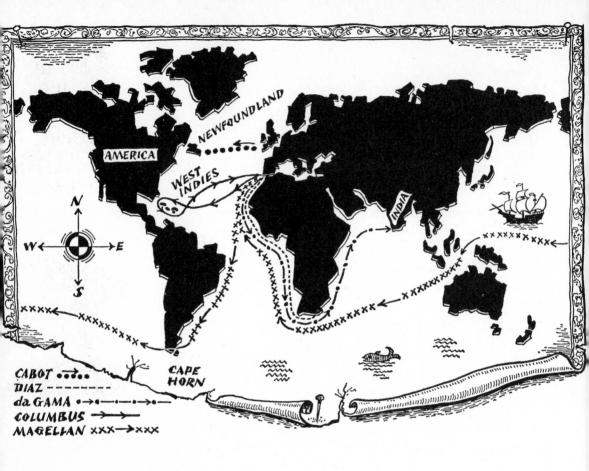

NEWFOUNDLAND

AMERICA

WEST
INDIES

INDIA

N
W   E
S

CAPE
HORN

CABOT ·····
DIAZ -------
da GAMA ·-·-·-
COLUMBUS →
MAGELLAN ×××→×××

CHAPTER I

Christopher Columbus

COLUMBUS

The voyages of discovery of the 15th and 16th century explorers are amongst the most important and exciting events in history. Look carefully at this map and you will see to where some of these explorers sailed.

In 1487 a Portuguese sailor named Bartholomew Diaz explored the coast of Africa. He discovered the Cape of Good Hope. Then Vasco da Gama, another Portuguese, went even further. He sailed round the Cape in 1498 and reached India. In the North you can see how John Cabot sailed from England and discovered Newfoundland. In 1519 a Portuguese sea captain, Ferdinand Magellan, began a voyage which was to be the first journey round the world. Magellan himself was killed, but his crew completed the voyage.

All these were wonderful achievements, but one voyage was more important than any. In 1492 Christopher Columbus sailed from Spain and discovered America.

DIAZ

Columbus was born in Genoa, a seaport on the Mediterranean Sea. When he was a small boy Columbus often walked by the quay. Valuable cargoes of silks and spices were unloaded

DA GAMA

there. These had been brought from Eastern countries like India. At that time there was no Suez Canal. The goods had to be carried by camel trains from the Red Sea to the Mediterranean Sea. This meant that the Arabs could make the merchants pay heavy taxes before they allowed them to cross the desert. It was because of this that explorers like Bartholomew Diaz and Vasco da Gama tried to find a new sea route to the East.

Columbus became a sailor when he was still only a boy. After some years at sea he went to live in Lisbon, the capital of Portugal. In the 15th century the Portuguese were the finest sailors in the world. Columbus was able to learn how to steer by the stars. He saw many new maps which had been drawn. He also learned how to use the sailors' compass which always pointed to the north.

In the 15th century people knew that the world was round and not flat. Columbus thought about this carefully. He believed that it should be possible to sail west instead of east and reach India more quickly.

If you look at a globe of the world you will see why Columbus was able to work out this plan. At that time, however, no one knew how large the world was. Nor did any one know about America.

For months Columbus thought about his plan. He knew that if he was to sail across the Atlantic he would need money to buy ships and to pay his crews. He was not a rich man and he could not carry out his scheme without help. At first he went to the King of Portugal. The Portuguese were not interested. They believed that their idea of sailing round the Cape of Good Hope was much better. Then Columbus explained his scheme to Ferdinand and Isabella, the King and Queen of Spain. They listened carefully to what he said and promised to consider his plan. For seven years they kept him waiting. At last Columbus lost all patience. He set off to speak to the King of France. When the Spaniards realized what he was doing messengers were sent to stop him. Columbus was promised the ships he needed.

FERDINAND

ISABELLA

Ferdinand and Isabella, with the help of a group of wealthy merchants, provided enough money for three ships. They were the *Santa Maria*, the *Pinta*, and the *Nina*. Even when he had the ships Columbus found it difficult to get crews. When they heard that Columbus intended to sail westwards sailors refused to join the ships. Many ordinary seamen still believed that the world was flat. They also spoke of monsters which swallowed up boats and their crews. To make enough men, convicts were freed from gaol if they promised to sail.

In September 1492 the three ships left harbour. They had begun what was to be the most important sea voyage of all time.

These ships were clumsily built, and were quite small—about the size of Thames pleasure steamers. In the open sea they rocked uncomfortably from side to side. On board the sailors' lives were very hard. The only food was coarse bread with salt meat or pork. After weeks at sea the drinking water turned foul. Cramped in the wet, smelly holds the men soon began to grumble. With only the empty sea before them they became afraid. As the time dragged by angry mutterings spread. It took all Columbus's skill as a captain to stop the men mutinying.

Each day Columbus looked for land. Once the captain of the *Pinta* called out that he could see an island. Excitedly the men crowded against the sides. To their disappointment they saw that it was only a bank of clouds. However, they had not many more days to wait. One morning flocking sea birds could be seen. Strange pieces of carved wood drifted past the boats. Suddenly the seaman on watch cried out, "Land ahoy". This time there was no mistake. There really was a shore ahead.

The island they were approaching was only small; today it is called Watling Street. Groups of brown-skinned natives stood watching as the Spanish ships drew near. Columbus ordered the sailors to drop anchor. Then putting on his finest uniform he was rowed ashore.

At the sight of these strange white men the natives fled in terror. From behind trees and rocks they watched as Columbus raised the Spanish flag. The first colony in the New World had been claimed for the King and Queen of Spain.

Columbus went on to discover more islands. He sailed as far as Cuba and Haiti. All the time he was convinced that he had reached Asia. For the rest of his life he never thought otherwise. That is why we call these islands the West Indies and why all the natives of America are called Indians.

Columbus left a party in the West Indies and returned to Spain. Wherever he went he was received as a hero. Ferdinand and Isabella came to meet him and he was welcomed to the royal court. The people of Spain looked with wonder at the strange plants and birds he had brought. Even more astonishing were the natives who were led through the Spanish streets. Some merchants noticed that he had brought no gold or spices. This did not worry Columbus for he was sure that they would be found on his next voyage.

In 1493 Columbus sailed again. On this voyage he had far more ships and hundreds of Spaniards wanted to go with him. When they reached the islands Columbus discovered that the men left behind were dead. They had tried to ill-treat the natives and had been killed. Time was to show that this was only the beginning of Spanish cruelty to the natives.

Columbus began to build settlements like this shown in the picture. They were meant as homes for the Spaniards and as a defence against Indians. Other islands were discovered and Columbus was made governor of them all. Unfortunately although Columbus was a fine sailor he was a poor governor. The Spanish settlers grew tired of his rules. At last they refused to obey him and sent him home in chains. Although the King and Queen freed him it was clear that Columbus was not the man to govern the new Spanish Empire.

Columbus made other voyages of discovery but when he finally returned to Spain he was almost forgotten. The man who had led the most famous voyage in history died without any of the honours he really deserved. Even the lands he discovered were not named after him. Only one country in the New World bears his name. That is Colombia in South America. America is named after another explorer, Amerigo Vespucci. He sailed to the mainland some years after Columbus's first discovery.

QUESTIONS

MAGELLAN

1. Why are these three explorers famous?
Bartholomew Diaz.
Vasco da Gama.
Ferdinand Magellan.

2. Answer these questions about Christopher Columbus.
   a. Where was Columbus born?
   b. What did he learn when he went to live in Portugal?
   c. How did Columbus plan to reach Asia?
   d. Which King did he first ask for help?
   e. Which King and Queen finally agreed to help him?
   f. What were the names of Columbus's three ships?
   g. In what year did Columbus discover America?
   h. Why are the natives of America called Indians?
   i. How do we know that Columbus was a poor governor?
   j. In what ways was Columbus unfortunate?

3. On a map of the world name the Red Sea and the Mediterranean Sea. Using different coloured crayons mark the routes taken by Bartholomew Diaz, Vasco da Gama, John Cabot, Ferdinand Magellan, and Christopher Columbus.

CABOT

4. Sea captains keep what are called log books. In these they write down the daily happenings.

Imagine that you were Columbus on the *Santa Maria*. Write a log for three different days. You can include in the log:
   Day 1. The day you sailed.
   Day 2. The day on which the men began to mutiny.
   Day 3. The day on which land was sighted.

5. See how quickly you can memorize this jingle (learned by many American children):

> In fourteen hundred and ninety-two
> Columbus sailed the ocean blue.

CHAPTER 2

The Conquest of Mexico

Christopher Columbus discovered America in 1492. After that many Spanish seamen explored the West Indies and the coast of America. One of the countries they discovered was Mexico. There the Spaniards were amazed to see people in the villages wearing gold ornaments. It was not long before plans were made to send an expedition to Mexico. A remarkable man was chosen to lead the expedition. His name was Hernando Cortes.

On Good Friday 1519, Cortes and 700 men landed in Mexico. They came ashore on a deserted beach. If you look at an atlas you will see where this beach was. The town of Vera Cruz, which is Spanish for "True Cross", stands there today.

A number of different Indian tribes lived in Mexico. They were all ruled by a race of people called the Aztecs. The Aztecs had built a great capital called Mexico City. They lived there under their chief, Montezuma.

Cortes and his men had not been in Mexico long before messengers came to them from Montezuma. The Aztec chief sent presents made of gold and silver. At the same time he ordered the Spaniards not to come to his capital.

Once he had seen the presents Cortes knew that the Aztecs must be very wealthy. He decided to ignore Montezuma's order. Plans were made to march to Mexico City.

When Cortes's men heard this many of them were afraid. If they moved away from the coast they could easily be surrounded. They began to talk of sailing away. Cortes acted immediately. He ordered the destruction of all the boats except one. Then he told his men that he had left that boat for any of them who were cowards. He gave these cowards permission to leave, but no one did. A few days later the Spaniards began their march towards Mexico City.

Led by Cortes, the Spaniards marched inland. It was not long before some of the Indian tribes began to attack. These natives had no chance. They were only armed with bows and arrows and wooden swords. The Spaniards wore metal armour and carried guns. They also had a few cannon which terrified the Indians.

One tribe called the Tlascalans joined the Spaniards. For years the Aztecs had ruled over this tribe. They had forced them to pay taxes and made them into slaves. The Tlascalans thought that the Spaniards would help them to get their revenge.

17

CORTES

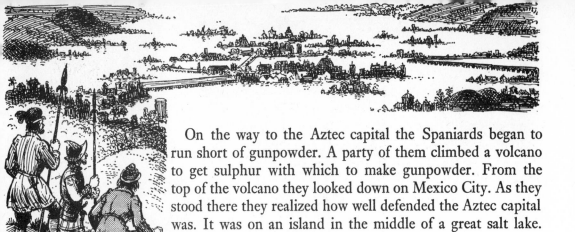

On the way to the Aztec capital the Spaniards began to run short of gunpowder. A party of them climbed a volcano to get sulphur with which to make gunpowder. From the top of the volcano they looked down on Mexico City. As they stood there they realized how well defended the Aztec capital was. It was on an island in the middle of a great salt lake. The only way into the city was to cross one of three narrow causeways. Forts had been built at the entrance to each causeway.

When the Spaniards came down from the volcano they told Cortes what they had seen. As he listened he began to make plans to attack the forts.

Inside the city news had been brought to Montezuma that the Spaniards were near. The ruler of the Aztecs could not understand how Cortes had reached his capital. He thought that the Spaniards must have been sent by the gods. Montezuma gave orders that the strange white men were to be allowed to enter the city. He even gave them a palace in which to live.

Cortes had not been in Mexico City long before he was invited to meet Montezuma. The Spanish leader was taken to one of the Aztec temples. Cortes was a brave man but as he approached the temple he was horrified. A young man was being dragged across the floor. The temple priests held the captive across a block of polished stone. Slowly the high priest cut open the man's breast. Then with savage cries he tore out the victim's heart.

Cortes had to turn away. This was the first time he had

MONTEZUMA

ever seen a human being sacrificed to an idol. Later he was to learn that the victim's body was given to the man who had captured him. It was then prepared as a meal by that man for his friends.

Although Cortes was an adventurer, he was a Christian. He believed that it was his duty to convert the Aztecs to Christianity. He tried to show the Aztecs that their idols were false gods. When Montezuma saw how the Spaniards were treating the temple gods he grew angry. Cortes realized that he and his men were in a dangerous position. The Spanish leader decided to hold Montezuma as a hostage. It was a clever move for it meant that the Aztecs would not dare to attack.

Then Cortes began to seize as much gold as he could. The Aztecs watched angrily as the Spaniards stole their treasure. At last they felt that Montezuma had betrayed them. The whole Aztec army rose against the Spaniards. When Montezuma tried to stop them they stoned him to death.

Cortes knew that the position was desperate. Thousands of Aztec warriors surrounded his small army. He ordered a wooden bridge to be built. As night fell he and his men crept towards the water front. Suddenly the Aztecs attacked. Desperately the Spaniards fought their way down the causeway. Man after man was killed. Some, laden with gold, fell into the lake and were drowned. Many were clubbed to death by the Aztecs. That night Cortes lost most of his men. Only a few were able to reach safety.

A lesser man than Cortes would have accepted defeat. Instead he withdrew to the coast to gather another army. This time he had 500 Spaniards, but in addition over 10,000 Indians who hated the rule of the Aztecs. He also built canoes with which to cross the lake.

With this army he marched on Mexico City again. His plan was to surround it and starve the Aztecs out. At the same time his cannons smashed the temples and palaces of the beautiful city.

The Spaniards attacked at all the weak points, but the Aztecs drove them off. Any Spaniards who were captured were sacrificed on the city walls. Cortes and his men had to watch helplessly as their comrades screamed with the terrible tortures.

Inside the city, however, the Aztecs were starving. Dead warriors rotted in the streets. The air was filled with the smell of their bodies. At last Cortes knew that he could attack. With their Indian allies the Spaniards charged into the city.

Temples and palaces were ruined. The Aztec priests and warriors were murdered in the streets. When the battle was over the great Aztec empire was destroyed for ever.

Mexico became part of the Spanish Empire. The Aztecs were made into slaves. Their gold and silver was loaded into treasure ships. The great wealth of the Aztecs was to help to make Spain into the richest country in Europe during the 16th century.

QUESTIONS

1. a. When did Cortes land in Mexico?
   b. How many men had he?
   c. Who was the chief of the Aztecs?
   d. How could Cortes tell that the Aztecs were very wealthy?
   e. Why did Cortes destroy his own boats?
   f. Why were the Spaniards able to defeat the Indian tribes?
   g. Why did some of the Spaniards climb the volcano?
   h. Why did some of the Aztecs rise against Cortes?
   i. What happened to Montezuma?
   j. What did Cortes do after he had been driven from Mexico City?
   k. Describe how Cortes finally defeated the Aztecs.
   l. Why did Spain become so rich in the 16th century?

2. The Aztecs did not have an alphabet like ours. Instead their writing was in pictures. Send a picture message from Montezuma to Cortes telling him not to come to Mexico City.

3. Look carefully at the pictures of the temple and the Aztec gods. Then imagine that you were a Spaniard who had returned home. Write a short story describing what you saw to your friends.

4. Discuss with your teacher how the Spaniards defeated the famous Incas of Peru.

GROUP WORK

Using coloured paper make a large picture of an Aztec temple. Show the way in which it was beautifully decorated and some of the statues of the idols.

CHAPTER 3

The Protestant Reformation

LUTHER

One of the most important events in history took place in the 16th century. It was called the Protestant Reformation.

Until 1517 most Christians in Europe were Roman Catholics. In that year a German monk named Martin Luther wrote an amazing document, attacking certain practices of the Catholic Church. In later writings he returned to the attack, declaring that there were priests who were idle, and some who could hardly read or write. Others were wealthy while the people in their parishes were very poor. Luther also said that the leaders of the Catholic Church, and even the Pope himself, did not always act like Christians.

Many other men supported Martin Luther. They were called Protestants because they were protesting at what was wrong with the Catholic Church.

HENRY VIII

News of the Reformation soon reached England. In 1517 Henry VIII was the King of England. At that time Henry was still a handsome young man. He was very popular with his people who called him Bluff King Hal. They admired his skill as a huntsman and his ability at tennis and archery.

Henry was also a clever scholar. He knew why the Reformation had taken place. Even so he supported the Pope at first and wrote a book opposing the Protestants. The Pope was so pleased with this that he gave Henry the title of Defender of the Faith. To this day some of our coins still have written on them Fid. Def. or F.D. This is short for the Latin "Fidei Defensor", Defender of the Faith, although now it does not mean the Catholic Church.

Although Henry opposed the Protestants it was partly because of him that the Reformation reached England. Henry had married his brother's widow. She was a Spanish noblewoman named Katharine of Aragon. Henry and Katharine had one daughter named Mary. Their other children had died when they were still babies. Henry wanted a son to succeed him, for he believed that England needed a strong king as a ruler. It was at the time when Henry was thinking of the need for another wife that he fell in love with Anne Boleyn. Anne Boleyn was a young lady of the royal court. In this picture she is walking behind Queen Katharine.

ANNE BOLEYN

Henry made up his mind to divorce Katharine, and marry Anne. This was to prove very difficult, for the Catholic Church rarely allowed divorces.

King Henry knew that only one man could help him. That was Thomas Wolsey, his chief minister or Lord Chancellor as he was called. Wolsey was the son of an Ipswich butcher. He was a man of great intelligence and ability. Not only was he Lord Chancellor, he was also a Cardinal, a high rank in the Catholic Church. In this picture Wolsey is talking to a group of leading nobles. The building in the background is Hampton Court. This was the huge palace which Wolsey had built for himself.

Cardinal Wolsey knew how difficult it would be for him to arrange a divorce for Henry. He also knew that he did not dare to fail the King.

KATHARINE OF ARAGON

CARDINAL WOLSEY

The Pope was in a very awkward position when he was asked to grant Henry a divorce. Katharine of Aragon was the aunt of Charles V, the King of Spain. At that time the King of Spain was one of the most powerful rulers in Europe. The Pope could not risk annoying him.

It was decided to hold a trial to decide whether Henry should be given a divorce. The Pope gave orders that the trial was to last as long as possible. He did not want to make any decision.

When she was brought before the judges, Katharine pleaded with them not to allow the divorce. She could not understand why Henry had begun to hate her. The King knew that Katharine had always been a good wife, but he showed her no pity. He intended to marry Anne Boleyn no matter how much Katharine suffered.

The court kept Henry waiting for months. At last he lost patience. Angrily he dismissed Wolsey from his post as Lord Chancellor. He let him keep only one important post, that of Archbishop of York. Not long after, however, Wolsey was accused of treason and brought to London. On the journey to the capital, Cardinal Wolsey, by then an old man, was taken ill. He was carried into Leicester Abbey where he died.

Although Wolsey was dead King Henry had still not obtained his divorce. The King then took the advice of the new Lord Chancellor. His name was Thomas Cromwell. Cromwell worked out a plan to help the King. He told Henry to make himself the Head of the Church in England. Henry

saw that Cromwell's idea was perfect. England would still be a Catholic country but the King, and not the Pope, would be the leader of the Church. It also meant that he could divorce himself, for he would no longer need the Pope's permission.

In this way King Henry obtained his divorce and married Anne Boleyn. Far more important was the fact that the Pope no longer had authority in England. Gradually the Protestant Reformation spread over the country. Soon after King Henry died, the Church of England, and not the Roman Catholic Church, was the most important church in England.

Up to this time Church services had usually been in Latin. Now the King encouraged translations of the Bible and Prayer Book into English, and this was a great help to the many people who did not understand Latin. There were still many who could not read, even in English, but at least they could now follow what the priest was saying.

QUESTIONS

1. a. Which German monk played an important part in starting the Protestant Reformation?
   b. When did it begin?
   c. What did this monk say was wrong with the Roman Catholic Church?
   d. Why were the reformers called Protestants?
   e. Why was King Henry VIII given the title "Defender of the Faith"?
   f. There were two main reasons why Henry VIII wanted a divorce. What were they?
   g. Who was Cardinal Wolsey?
   h. Why was the Pope reluctant to grant a divorce?
   i. What happened to Wolsey when he failed to get the divorce?
   j. What scheme did Thomas Cromwell suggest to Henry VIII?

THOMAS
CROMWELL

2. If you look at different coins you will see words written in Latin in a shortened form. Try to find out what these words mean.

3. Visit your school library. Find out how many wives Henry VIII had, what their names were, and what happened to them.

4. Discuss with your teacher:
   a. Who is the present Pope?
   b. Who is the present head of the Church of England?
   c. What are the main differences between the Church of England and the Roman Catholic Church?

5. If possible try to visit Hampton Court.

CHAPTER 4

The Dissolution of the Monasteries

You have already learned how the monks lived in the monasteries during the Middle Ages. They spent much of their time praying to God. They taught children and looked after the sick. Many of them, like these in the picture, gave food to beggars and accommodation to travellers.

At the beginning of the 16th century there were about 12,000 monks and over 500 monasteries in England. However, they were not as useful as they had once been. More schools had been built. Many towns had inns and it was only in the wild north of England that travellers still depended on the monasteries. After the printing press was invented there was no need for books to be written out by hand. Copying and decorating books had been one of the most important duties in many monasteries.

Some of the larger monasteries were very wealthy. They possessed great sums of money. In their churches were valuable gold and silver ornaments. Even more important were the vast areas of land which they owned.

It was these riches that led Thomas Cromwell, the Lord Chancellor who had helped Henry to get his divorce, to suggest another scheme to the King. As Cromwell explained, if the King closed the monasteries he would be able to confiscate their wealth. Henry VIII needed money badly and he listened eagerly to the Lord Chancellor's plan.

Cromwell sent his men to visit the monasteries and report on the way the monks lived. Some of these reports were good. There were monasteries where the monks still gave their lives to worshipping God and helping the poor. As the reports showed, this was not true of them all. There were far too many monasteries where the monks took little interest in religion. King Henry was able to read accounts of abbots who spent their days hunting and of monks who lived in luxury. It was reports like these that gave him the excuse he needed.

Henry VIII and Cromwell soon acted. In 1536 and later in 1540, orders were given for the monasteries to be closed. All over England the King's officers rode out to the monasteries. Everything of value was removed. Gold and silver ornaments were taken away. Lead was stripped from the roofs. Most important of all was the land which had belonged to the monasteries. This was sold and the money went to the King.

The monks were forced to leave the monasteries but it is not true that many of them suffered. Most were given pensions, although these were sometimes only small. Many monks became priests and some of the abbots were made into important bishops.

GLASTONBURY ABBEY

The deserted monasteries soon became ruins. They were often pulled down by farmers and townsmen and the stones used for houses. All over England these ruined monasteries can still be seen. Many of them like Tintern Abbey, Fountains Abbey, and Glastonbury, show very clearly how large and beautiful the monasteries sometimes were. Some of the deserted monasteries like Tewkesbury and Malmesbury became part of the town churches. Chester and Durham are now part of the cathedrals.

It is always interesting to find out whether there were any monasteries near to your school and to discover what happened to them.

QUESTIONS

1. Why was it that the monasteries were not as useful in the 16th century as they had been in the Middle Ages?
2. Why did King Henry VIII dissolve the monasteries?
3. What happened to the monks after the monasteries were dissolved?
4. Read again the chapter on Monasteries in Book 1. Make notes of the main buildings. Then try to visit the ruins of a monastery. Make sketches and a plan of what remains. Copy these into your class book.

CHAPTER 5

Sir Francis Drake

DRAKE

We saw in Chapter 2 how the Spaniards had defeated the Aztecs and Incas and seized their gold mines. Now look carefully at map A of South and Central America. The Spaniards brought the gold from Peru to the Panama Isthmus. From there it was taken by pack mule and loaded on ships to be sent to Spain (B). These Spanish treasure ships carried millions of pounds worth of gold and silver. In the 16th century Spain became the richest country in Europe.

News of the great wealth on board these ships soon spread. Pirates began to attack the slow-moving galleons as they sailed away from the West Indies. Among these pirates were many English sailors who were ready to risk their lives against the Spaniards. Probably the most famous of them all was a young Devon sea captain. His name was Francis Drake.

PANAMA

TO SPAIN

PERU

PACIFIC OCEAN

ATLANTIC OCEAN

(A)

SHIPS TO SPAIN

ISTHMUS OF PANAMA

PANAMA

SHIPS FROM PERU

(B)

Drake had once traded peacefully with the Spaniards. He had only become their enemy because of Spanish treachery. On one occasion they had robbed him of his cargo and murdered many of his crew. From that day he had sworn to have his revenge. The Spaniards soon learned to hate the name of El Draco.

On one voyage to Panama, Drake had climbed a tree to look out across the narrow neck of land. From the top of this tree he saw the Pacific Ocean for the first time. He also saw Spanish treasure ships at anchor, and teams of mules carrying gold to the boats which waited on the Atlantic side of the isthmus.

As he climbed down Drake vowed that one day he would sail into the Pacific and raid the Spaniards.

Drake's chance soon came. In 1577 he was invited to meet a group of merchants and businessmen. With a globe of the explored world before them they showed Drake where they wanted him to sail. At that time no one had discovered Australia. The merchants wanted him to search for a vast unknown southern continent which was supposed to exist. It was thought that the only way to reach it was to sail down the coast of South America and through the Magellan Straits. These were the straits discovered by Ferdinand Magellan, the famous Portuguese explorer, in 1519.

As he stood looking at the globe Drake must have thought of the treasure ships in the Pacific Ocean.

In December 1577 five ships left Plymouth. At their head was the *Pelican*, closely followed by the *Elizabeth* and the *Marigold*. The two small supply ships were the *Swan* and the *Benedict*.

The 164 men who sailed with Drake did not know where they were going. Drake had told them that it was a voyage to Alexandria in the Mediterranean Sea. He knew that many of them would have been afraid to sail had they known the truth.

This is a picture of the inside of Drake's cabin. He had made a lot of money from his previous voyages. Now he could afford every possible luxury. Live chickens were carried so that he could have fresh meat. He ate off silver plates. He wore rich clothes and there were minstrels on board to entertain him.

Keeping well clear of the coast of Spain, the ships travelled slowly southwards. As they crossed the Equator the weather was unpleasantly hot. The men knew that they had been tricked. Many of them began to mutter amongst themselves. From the bridge Drake watched for any signs of trouble and gave orders for the ships to sail towards Brazil.

As the days passed the threats of mutiny grew. The main plotter was Thomas Doughty, one of the leading officers. When Drake was warned of this he could not believe it at first. Doughty had been his friend and Drake had trusted him. When even more evidence was found showing that Doughty was the ringleader, there was only one thing Drake could do. He ordered the ships to anchor off a deserted coast now called Port Saint Julian. There Doughty was tried. He was found guilty of mutiny against his captain. For that there was only one sentence. Early next morning Thomas Doughty was executed.

The ships sailed south towards the dreaded Magellan Straits. This was the passage which Magellan had discovered between the mainland of South America and the island of Tierra del Fuego. At that time it was thought to be the only way through to the Pacific Ocean.

At the entrance to the Straits the *Swan* and *Benedict* were broken up. The *Pelican* was given the name by which she will always be remembered, the *Golden Hind*.

The three remaining ships made towards the Straits. Towering mountains and threatening rocks lay in their path. For five hundred kilometres they would have to sail through some of the most dangerous seas in the world. Each day Drake and his captains looked anxiously at the sea and the rolling clouds. Luck was with them. The weather remained fine. For sixteen days they steered through the Straits. Then the three ships reached the Pacific Ocean. This was the ocean that Magellan had called the peaceful sea.

No sooner had Drake and his ships entered the Pacific Ocean than the weather changed. A violent storm blew up. Before the crashing waves the tiny boats were helpless. For a month the *Golden Hind* was driven south. Only Drake's brilliant seamanship kept his boat afloat. The *Marigold* was less fortunate. She disappeared with all hands. The *Elizabeth* survived and when the storm ended her captain tried to find the Golden Hind. For weeks they kept a constant look-out. When there was no sign of Drake, the captain of the *Elizabeth* decided to return to England. Of the five ships which had sailed from England only the *Golden Hind* was left in the Pacific.

During the storm Drake had been driven well south of Tierra del Fuego. He had discovered that it was only an island and not the great continent he had intended to explore. As soon as the wind dropped he turned north again to look for his other ships. When there was no sign of them he thought that they must have been sunk in the storm. He gave up the search but he did not return to England. Instead he set course for Panama. He intended to attack the Spanish treasure ships when they least expected him.

Slowly the *Golden Hind* sailed north up the coast of South America. There were a number of small fishing ports and in some of these Drake discovered Spanish boats. He raided them and took whatever gold and treasure they had on board.

Then one day they learned from a native that one of the greatest of the Spanish treasure ships, the *Cacafuego*, had only just left. Quickly Drake sailed after it. Soon they saw the great boat ahead of them. No one on board the Spanish

ship realized that Drake was in the Pacific. Even when the
Golden Hind drew near they did not suspect danger. Suddenly
Drake fired his cannon across the *Cacafuego*'s prow. The
Spanish captain watched with astonishment as Drake ordered
him to surrender. The Spaniard looked at the English guns
and he knew that he had no choice. With drawn swords
Drake and his men leaped on to the *Cacafuego*. Helplessly
the Spaniards stood by as the English forced their way into
the ship's holds. Drake gazed with amazement at the treasure
chests stored below. There was more gold, silver, emeralds,
and pearls than the English had ever thought possible. They
could not have captured a richer prize.

After the capture of the *Cacafuego* the *Golden Hind* was loaded with treasure. Drake had to return to England. He knew that this would not be easy. If he went back the way he had come the Spaniards would be on the look-out. Drake decided to sail north. It was believed that there was a north-west passage round the top of North America.

As the heavily laden ship sailed northwards the weather got much colder. It was clear that they could not return that way. Drake turned south again and landed on the coast near to where the town of San Francisco now stands. Here the English sailors met a tribe of friendly Indians. These Indians thought that Drake was a god and almost worshipped him. The crew were able to rest and gather fresh food and water. Before he left Drake hammered a brass plate into a tree. This was discovered by accident in 1937.

Drake set sail west, towards the Spice Islands. They crossed the Pacific safely and landed in the islands for fresh water. As they were navigating a narrow channel between the islands the *Golden Hind* went aground. Immediately Drake ordered the crew to throw some of the guns and stores overboard.

He knew that the ship had to be lightened. Anxiously the crew waited until the *Golden Hind* slid into deep water.

Even then they were not safe. They had to find their way out of the islands for they had heard that a Portuguese fleet was approaching. With a man at the helm measuring the dangerous shoals, Drake edged the *Golden Hind* towards open sea. Then he set course towards the Indian Ocean and the long voyage back to England.

It was September 1580 before they finally reached England. They sailed up the English coast towards London. News of the vast treasure they were carrying went before them.

When the *Golden Hind* anchored in the Thames, Queen Elizabeth came aboard. It was on the deck of his famous ship that she knighted Sir Francis Drake. He had been the first Englishman to sail round the world.

QUESTIONS

1. a. Why was Spain the richest country in Europe in the 16th century?
   b. Why did Francis Drake hate the Spaniards?
   c. From where did Drake see the Pacific Ocean for the first time?
   d. On the day Drake saw the Pacific Ocean what else did he see?
   e. After whom are the Magellan Straits named?
   f. What were the names of the 5 ships which left Plymouth in December 1577?

QUEEN ELIZABETH

g. Why did Drake tell his men that they were sailing to the Mediterranean Sea?

k. Which land did they really intend to explore?

i. Why was Doughty executed?

j. What was the new name given to the *Pelican*?

k. Which of the ships was sunk by the storm in the Pacific?

l. What happened to the *Elizabeth*?

m. What was the name of the richest treasure ship that Drake raided?

n. What proof has been found that Drake landed near to where the town of San Francisco now stands?

o. When did Drake finally return to England?

2. On a map of the world mark Drake's route. Use your atlas and mark on the map:

Plymouth.

Port St Julian where Doughty was executed.

Tierra del Fuego and the Magellan Straits.

Where the *Cacafuego* was raided near the coast of Peru.

San Francisco.

The Spice Islands.

London.

3. In your own words describe the inside of Drake's cabin.

4. Imagine that you were a sailor on the *Golden Hind*. Write down the three events which you remember most. Explain why these were so important.

GROUP WORK

On a large outline map of the world mark in Drake's route. Draw or find pictures of Drake's ships. Also draw pictures of the most important happenings. Put these on to the map to show the adventures that Drake had.

CHAPTER 6

Mary, Queen of Scots

MARY QUEEN OF SCOTS

In 1542, King James V of Scotland died. The heir to the throne was his daughter Mary. She was only one week old. This meant that her mother had to act as regent and rule the country for her.

At that time England and Scotland were two separate countries. The King of England, Henry VIII, wanted to unite them so that he could rule both. He made plans for Mary to marry his son Edward. The Scots lords refused to agree to this. Henry himself did not live much longer but the English still sent an army to force the Scots to accept the marriage. Mary's mother was French, and it was decided that the safest plan was for the young Queen to go to France. There she could be brought up at the French royal court.

This is a picture of the French court in the 16th century. It was the finest in Europe. Mary grew up to be a beautiful and talented woman. She was taught to dance gracefully

and to play musical instruments. Expert needlewomen gave her lessons in embroidery. Noble ladies showed her how to talk and act like a Queen.

In 1558 she married the Dauphin, the eldest son of the King of France. A year later the King died. This meant that when she was only seventeen Mary was Queen of France and Scotland. It seemed as if she was the most fortunate woman in the world.

Soon afterwards her good fortune began to change.

Two years later, when Mary was nineteen, her husband died. The French soon showed that they did not want her as their Queen. She decided to return to Scotland.

On a wet, foggy day in August 1561, Mary came ashore at the port of Leith. Hardly anyone knew that she was coming. There were only a few lords on the quayside to welcome their Queen. However, news of her return quickly spread. When she arrived in Edinburgh the streets were crowded with cheering people.

Mary found Scotland very different from France. The weather was much colder. The nobles at Holyrood Palace were far more serious than the courtiers she had known in France. Also when Mary first went to France the Scots had been mainly Roman Catholic. She came back to a country which was becoming Protestant. One of the most important men in the country was the religious reformer, John Knox.

In this picture Knox is being presented to Mary at Holyrood Palace. He showed her no respect. Mary was a Catholic, and Knox hated the Roman Catholic religion.

At first Mary ruled well. She listened to the advice of her ministers, and although she remained a Catholic she tried not to offend John Knox and his followers.

In 1565 she married a Scots noble named Lord Darnley. It was not long before she realized what a mistake this marriage had been. Darnley was a coward and a drunkard. He was incapable of helping Mary to govern Scotland. As the months passed Mary became more and more unhappy.

JOHN KNOX

She began to rely on the advice of her private secretary. He was an Italian named David Rizzio. When Darnley heard that she preferred Rizzio's company to his, he became bitterly angry. With a group of friends he planned to murder the Italian.

One evening in March 1566, Mary and her ladies-in-waiting were listening to Rizzio playing his violin. Suddenly the door burst open. Darnley and his followers pushed their way in. The women stood terrified. Rizzio clung pitifully to the Queen but Darnley's men dragged him away. Brutally they murdered him outside the door.

Mary never forgave Darnley for this. She now began to rely increasingly on the advice of another noble, the Earl of Bothwell. A few months after Rizzio's murder a mysterious explosion shocked the people of Edinburgh. Darnley was recovering from smallpox in a house at Kirk o' Fields, near to Edinburgh, when the house was blown up. Darnley must have been warned of the danger, for he tried to escape. As he ran into the garden he was caught and murdered.

Although it was never proved who had committed the crime, the Earl of Bothwell was the chief suspect. There were even rumours that Mary had helped to plan the murder. Most people refused to believe this.

The murder would have been forgotten, for Darnley was not popular. Then Mary made the worst possible mistake. She married the Earl of Bothwell. The Scottish people could not forgive her for this. Bothwell was disliked by both Catholics and Protestants, quite apart from the question of his guilt in the Darnley murder.

The Scots lords revolted against their Queen. The two armies met at Carberry Hill. The battle never began. When Mary saw how strong the opposing army was, she surrendered. The lords took her as a prisoner to Loch Leven Castle.

Mary had only been a prisoner for a few months when plans were made to free her. The escape was carefully planned. She was guided out of the castle by her sixteen-year-old page, Willie Douglas. No one heard them as they crept down to the shore. Swiftly she was rowed across the loch. On the

far side friends were waiting to meet her. She was given a horse and led to freedom.

Shortly afterwards Mary raised a new army. This was completely defeated at the Battle of Langside. Mary escaped and fled to England. There she asked her cousin Queen Elizabeth to protect her.

Queen Elizabeth allowed Mary to remain in England. For nineteen years she was kept in different castles. These included Sheffield, where she stayed for fourteen years, Bolton, Wakefield, and Tutbury.

Foolishly, however, Mary still mixed with many leading Catholics. Plots were hatched by some of these Catholics to make Mary the Queen of England. Because she was partly Tudor, they claimed that she had as good a right as Elizabeth. At first she did not take part in these conspiracies. Then in 1587 English spies discovered that Mary had taken part in a plan to make England into a Catholic country again.

This time Elizabeth was forced to order her arrest. Mary was tried and found guilty of treason. Elizabeth had no choice but to sign her death warrant. In 1587, Mary, Queen of Scots, was executed at Fotheringay Castle.

Although Mary had been executed, her son, James VI of Scotland, was to become King of England in 1603, for Elizabeth died without leaving any heirs to the throne.

QUESTIONS

1. Write a story of the life of Mary, Queen of Scots. Include in your story:
   a. Her life at the French court.
   b. Her return to Scotland.
   c. The murder of Rizzio.
   d. Her marriage to the Earl of Bothwell.
   e. Her defeat at the battle of Carberry.
   f. How she escaped from prison.
   g. Why she came to England and why at last Queen Elizabeth had to have her executed.

   If possible draw pictures to illustrate the story.

2. If you are Scottish discuss with your teacher the importance of the work of John Knox. Then write a short account of his life and work.

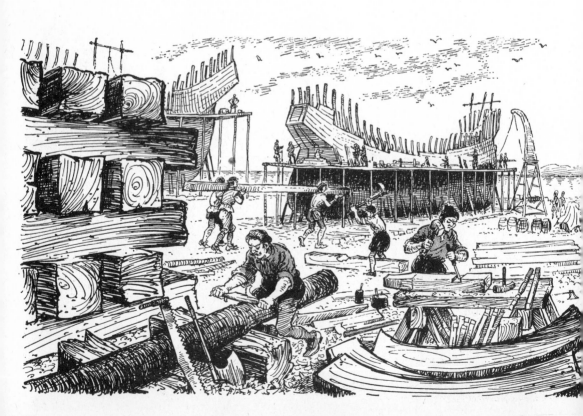

CHAPTER 7

The Spanish Armada

In the year 1587 every shipyard in Spain was busy. Philip II, the King of Spain, had given orders that the greatest fleet of all time was to be built. This Armada was intended to sail against England.

Philip II had two important reasons for wanting to invade England. The first was that the Spanish treasure ships were often attacked by English sailors like Sir Francis Drake. Drake had already destroyed many Spanish ships. The second reason was religious. Philip was a Roman Catholic and he felt bound to do everything he could to spread his faith. Queen Elizabeth and most English people were Protestants, and Elizabeth had ordered the execution of a famous Catholic, Mary, Queen of Scots.

There were to be over one hundred and thirty ships in the Armada. Leading the fleet were huge galleons, the strongest of the Spanish ships. The ships with both sails and oars were called galleasses. These boats were rowed by convicts who had been sentenced to be chained to the oars.

A great Spanish nobleman named the Duke of Medina-Sidonia was put in command of the Armada. In this picture he is watching some of his soldiers going on board the ships. The Duke was not a sailor and had never commanded a ship before. His orders were to sail to the Low Countries, which we now call Belgium and Holland. There he was to pick up another Spanish army led by the Duke of Parma.

In 1588 the Armada was ready to sail. Spies had brought word to England that it was being prepared. Queen Elizabeth ordered every available fighting ship to sail against the Spaniards. Altogether the English had 190 ships in their fleet.

Around the coast of England these vessels were prepared for war. In this picture a group of sailors are busily loading one ship. The cannon balls weighed about 14 kilogrammes each. They were used in cannons like the heavy gun being dragged along the quayside. A gun like that could fire almost two kilometres. It was not very accurate because the ball was rarely the right size for the barrel. Smaller cannons were also used. Instead of cannon balls some of the guns fired spread shot on to the enemy decks.

The English fleet gathered at Plymouth. In command was Lord Howard of Effingham. Under him he had some of the finest sailors in the world. They included Francis Drake, John Hawkins, and Martin Frobisher.

LORD HOWARD

FROBISHER

HAWKINS

On July 19th, 1588, the Spanish Armada was sighted. Captain Fleming, the captain of the ship that had spotted the Armada, hurried to Plymouth to warn Lord Howard and Francis Drake. There is a famous story that he found the two commanders playing bowls on Plymouth Hoe. Drake listened to the excited captain. Calmly he replied, "There is time for us to finish the game and still beat the Spaniards". As he spoke Drake must have been planning the best way to attack the Spaniards.

ENGLISH GALLEON   SPANISH GALLEÓN

During that night and early the following morning the
English fleet sailed out of Plymouth towards the open sea.
The sailors standing on deck looked with wonder at the
Armada. As the picture shows the Spanish admiral had
arranged his ships in the shape of a crescent. Their weakest
ships were in the centre. Their most powerful were either
at the front or on the wings. Drake and Howard knew that
it would be very difficult to attack this formation.

Another picture shows an important point. The turrets
on the English ships were lower than on the Spanish. This
made the English ships easier to control. Even so the English
did not dare to get too close to the Spanish. There were many
soldiers on board the enemy ships waiting for an opportunity
to use their grappling irons. Drake had to fire his cannons
from a distance. This meant that the cannon balls were less
accurate and did not do a lot of damage.

Slowly the great Armada drifted up the English Channel.
At last they reached the port of Calais and there they stopped.
The Spanish admiral expected the Duke of Parma to be
ready with his army, but Parma had been unable to arrive
on time.

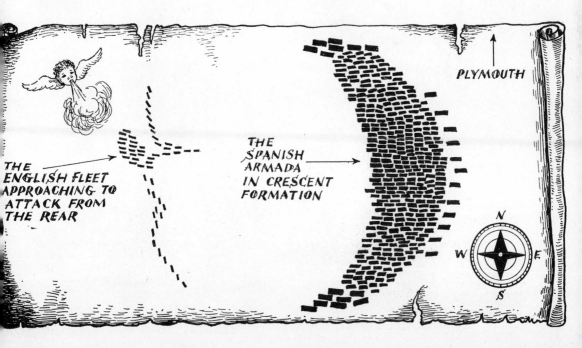

THE ENGLISH FLEET APPROACHING TO ATTACK FROM THE REAR

THE SPANISH ARMADA IN CRESCENT FORMATION

PLYMOUTH

The English fleet waited outside Calais harbour. Drake decided to send in fire-ships. These were old ships filled with anything that would burn. That night the Spaniards on watch saw the blazing ships drifting towards them. Immediately orders were given for every Spanish ship to weigh anchor. Panic-stricken, the Spanish captains steered their ships towards the mouth of the harbour. Not one ship was damaged by fire but the tightly packed crescent was broken. The English were waiting as the Spaniards came into the open sea.

The English fleet was ordered to attack. With their cannons blazing Drake and his men swept down on the Spaniards.

Their ships were much faster and far easier to control. The great galleons could not turn quickly enough to avoid the volleys of shots. As the Spanish admiral saw his vessels being sunk he knew that the crescent must be reformed. Very skilfully the Spanish captains managed to do this, but not before they had lost many of their best boats. Then in the heat of the battle the English found themselves running out of ammunition. Seizing their chance the Spaniards fled towards the Low Countries.

Although many Spanish ships had escaped, the great Armada was defeated. There was no longer any risk of the Spanish soldiers invading England. All that the Spanish admiral could do was to try to get back to Spain. This would be difficult, for the Duke of Medina-Sidonia dared not return by the Channel. The only way back was round the coast of Scotland.

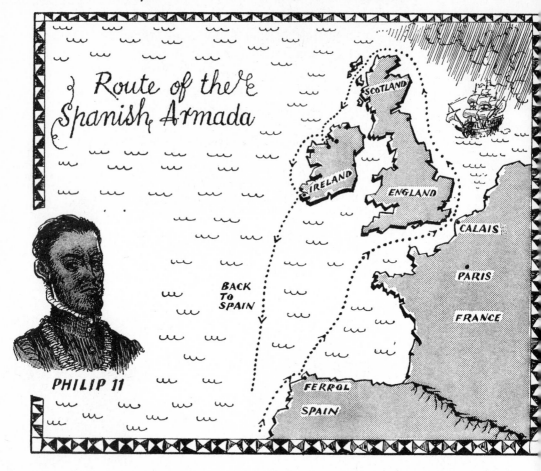

Route of the Spanish Armada

SCOTLAND

IRELAND

ENGLAND

CALAIS

PARIS

FRANCE

BACK TO SPAIN

FERROL

SPAIN

PHILIP II

This map shows from where the Armada came and how it returned to Spain. The seas off the northern coast of Scotland are very dangerous. On the terrible retreat many ships were sunk. Some were wrecked off Scotland and Ireland. Others just sank in the stormy seas.

Of the 130 ships which had left Spain only 53 returned. The English sea-dogs had won a great victory.

QUESTIONS

1. a. Who was the King of Spain in 1587?
   b. Why was the Armada prepared?
   c. What were the strongest Spanish ships called?
   d. What was a galleasse?
   e. Who was in command of the Armada?
   f. How many English ships were there?
   g. Who was in command of the English fleet?
   h. Which English captain first spotted the Armada?
   i. Why was it difficult for Drake to attack the Armada?
   j. How did the English force the Spanish out of Calais harbour?
   k. Why were some of the Spanish ships able to escape to the Low Countries?
   l. How many ships returned to Spain?

2. On a map show the route taken by the Armada. Mark in: Spain, Portugal, Plymouth, where the Armada was first sighted, Calais, the Low Countries, the voyage round Scotland and Ireland.

3. Draw or trace a Spanish galleon and an English ship. Explain the differences between the two.

4. There is an exciting poem called *Drake's Drum* by Henry Newbolt. Copy this into your book and see how much of it you can learn.

5. Discuss with your teacher the search for the Spanish treasure ship which has gone on for many years in Tobermory Bay in Scotland.

Also discuss what is meant by "treasure trove".

CHAPTER 8

Tudor Houses

This is a picture of a Tudor house. It would have been built at some time during the 16th century. If you look carefully at the picture you will see that the bottom part of the house was built of bricks. This brickwork kept the wooden beams off the damp ground. The main framework of the house was

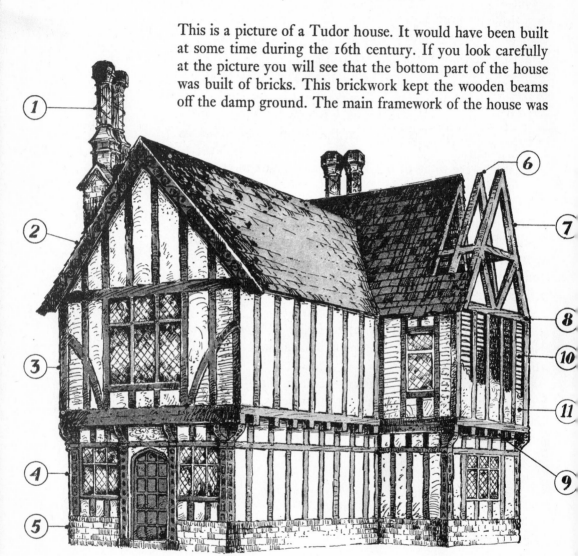

1 CHIMNEY
2 GABLE WITH CARVED
  BARGE BOARDS
3 PRINCIPAL POSTS
4 CARVED ANGLE POSTS

5 BRICK OR STONE WALL
6 RAFTERS
7 PRINCIPAL RAFTERS
8 TIE-BEAM
9 CEILING RAFTERS

10 LATHS OF HAZEL CALLED
   WATTLE, TO WHICH DAUB
   OR CLAY IS STUCK, IT IS
   THEN COVERED WITH-
11 PLASTER

made of great oak beams. The space in between this wooden frame was filled with wattle and daub. These houses were built so that the upper storey jutted out over the lower storey. This added strength to the building.

Although large Tudor houses had glass windows, the actual panes were only small because glass was expensive. The window frames themselves were large, for people in the 16th century were fond of as much light as possible in their houses. The roofs were usually made of brick tiles.

The Tudors were very proud of their houses. As this picture shows the doorways and roof gables were often beautifully carved. If you look at the chimneys you will see how attractive they were.

Not all Tudor houses were made of wood. Many of them were built of brick, or of stone like this one. Look closely at this house, particularly at the doorways, the windows, and the

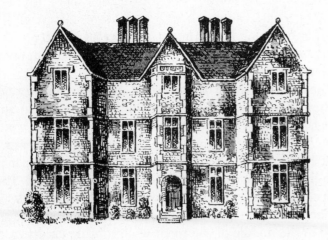

chimneys. You may know of Tudor houses near to your home which look like this, or like the half-timbered house in the first picture.

A large Tudor house had a number of different rooms. This is a picture of a parlour, the small private room used by the family.

The floor was made of stone slabs and covered with rushes. If these were not changed often they soon began to smell. Bunches of lavender and rosemary were kept in the window bays. These helped to sweeten the air. Wallpaper was not used during the 16th century. Instead the walls were panelled with light oak. As you can see the fireplace was large. In the 16th century logs, and not coal, were used to warm the houses.

There was not much furniture in Tudor houses. The small table in the middle of the room was probably used as a card table. The two large chairs and the chest were made of wood and attractively carved. The children had to sit on the wooden form and stool. Sometimes cushions were put on the chairs to make them more comfortable.

This is a picture of a bedroom in a 16th century house. As you can see the floor was made of wooden boards. The walls were panelled with different coloured woods. The ceiling was made of plaster and had an attractive pattern on it.

The only furniture in this room was a chest and an enormous four poster bed. This bed was very beautifully carved. Around the posts were heavy curtains which were drawn at night to keep out the draughts. The mattress rested on a strong rope mesh instead of the metal springs we have today. The mattress itself was made of feathers. The Tudors had linen sheets and comfortable pillows. Only the poor still used logs for pillows.

You will have noticed that dressing tables and wardrobes were not used. As there were no bathrooms in Tudor houses, people washed in basins like the one on the chest. The mirror in this room was made of polished metal and not of glass.

ANOTHER VIEW OF
A LONG GALLERY

This room was called the long gallery. It usually stretched the whole length of a house. The ladies walked in this room during bad weather and sometimes children were allowed to play games in it.

The long gallery was particularly useful when the family wanted to have a musical party. Most people in Tudor England were fond of music. They often entertained themselves by playing and singing. The group in this picture are playing a flute, a viol, and a recorder. The instrument which looks like a piano was called a virginal.

As you can see from this picture the long gallery was expensively decorated. The fireplaces were particularly attractive. They were surrounded by figures carved in wood and plaster. The Tudors also hung the few pictures they had in the long gallery.

You will probably have noticed that there were no carpets
in any of the rooms you have seen. Carpets were very dear.
Instead of putting them on the floor, people hung them from
the walls. In this way they helped to keep out the draughts
and make the rooms more colourful.

QUESTIONS

Most parts of Britain have either stone or black and white
16th century houses which can be visited by the public.

When you have read this chapter carefully you should
know what to look for in a Tudor house. Then arrange a
visit to one of these houses.

Look at the outside of the house and all the rooms. Make
notes of everything you see of interest, and make sketches
where possible.

When you return to school write a full account of the house
you have visited. Include as many pictures as you can.

CHAPTER 9

The Theatre

At the beginning of the 16th century people were still watching the miracle plays which had been popular in the Middle Ages. Miracle plays were always connected with religious events. There were plays about Herod and Noah, the Last Supper, and many other stories from the Bible.

This picture shows one of these plays being performed. The stage was set on a large wagon. It was erected high above the wheels so that there was space for a dressing room underneath. The words of the plays were simple. The audience had usually heard them so often that they knew what was going to be said. They loved to stand near to the stage cheering the heroes or booing such villains as Herod and Pontius Pilate. The onlookers also insisted that the plays were as real

as possible and great care had to be taken over making the scenery and costumes. This could be very difficult, particularly when the play was about the mouth of Hell or Jonah's whale.

Miracle plays had been acted for hundreds of years but by the end of the 16th century they were losing their popularity.

There were also groups of entertainers who travelled from town to town. These men were called strolling players. Many of them were very talented. As this picture shows they had to be able to sing, act, juggle, and do acrobatics.

In the 16th century it was illegal to wander around the country without definite work. These entertainers were regarded as vagabonds. They could be punished by being whipped or even branded on the face. The only way in which they could be safe from the law was for them to be employed by some wealthy nobleman.

79

It was towards the end of the 16th century that the theatre in London became really popular. In 1576 James Burbage, an actor, built the first English theatre. It was so popular that others soon followed it. This is a picture of the most famous of them all, the Globe. It was roughly circular in shape. There was no roof and the poorer members of the audience stood in an open yard. The wealthy sat in the galleries. A theatre like this could hold a thousand people.

Look carefully at the stage of this theatre. It was very cleverly designed. In the floor boards there was a trap door through which the characters could disappear if necessary. Above the stage there was a balcony. The actors could use this to pretend that they were on high buildings or hillsides. The Elizabethan theatre also had another platform above the balcony. This could be used if any part of the play was supposed to take place in heaven.

There were no changes of scene such as we have today. Instead signs were sometimes held up to tell the audience where the play was taking place.

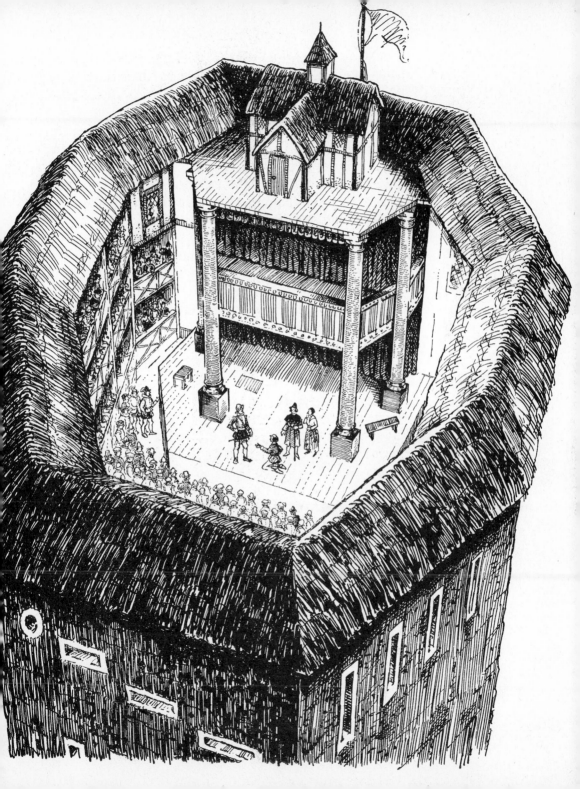

This is a picture of a play being performed. The actors were all men and any women's parts had to be taken by boys. Normally the actors wore their ordinary clothes but some characters had to wear costume.

As you can see the Elizabethan audiences intended to enjoy themselves. They ate, drank, sat on the stage, and sometimes even took part in the plays. They also demanded as many thrills as possible. Ghosts and murders were common in plays. To make these murders seem as real as possible the actors would sometimes use animals' blood and let it run on to the stage.

Theatre companies produced a number of plays each week and were always after new plays. During the 16th century there were a number of good playwrights but the greatest of them all was William Shakespeare.

William Shakespeare was born in Stratford-on-Avon. Not much is known about his early life except that his father was a prosperous glove merchant and William went to the local

SHAKESPEARE

grammar school. In 1582 he married Anne Hathaway. They had a daughter and then twins, a boy and a girl. At some time after the twins were born Shakespeare left for London.

When he was in London Shakespeare worked as an actor but he soon began to write plays. It was not long before his plays were famous. People laughed at his comedies. They were thrilled by his history plays. By the time he had begun to write his famous tragedies he was the most popular playwright in England. Shakespeare helped to make the theatre one of the favourite forms of entertainment of the 16th century.

William Shakespeare died in 1616 but his work will live for ever. Today plays like *Twelfth Night*, *Macbeth*, *Hamlet*, and *The Merchant of Venice*, to name only a few, are famous all over the world. Some of them have been made into films. He is remembered particularly in Stratford-on-Avon. There, a special memorial theatre is crowded every night with audiences watching plays which once delighted the people of Tudor England.

QUESTIONS

1. What were miracle plays?
2. Describe the miracle play which is being acted in the first picture.
3. Look carefully at the picture of a 16th century theatre. In what ways does it differ from a theatre today?
4. Write a short account in your own words of William Shakespeare. Try to find the names of some other plays which he wrote.

GROUP WORK

Make a model of a 16th century theatre.

CHAPTER 10

The Gunpowder Plot

FAWKES

CATESBY

In England today Catholics and Protestants live peacefully together. This has not always been so. During the 16th century England changed from being a Catholic to a Protestant country. During the reign of Queen Elizabeth I some Catholics had plotted against her. For this they were harshly treated. Catholics were fined if they did not attend a Protestant church. Also it was illegal for Catholic priests to live in England.

In 1603 Queen Elizabeth died and James I succeeded her. The Catholics soon realized that he also intended to persecute them.

In May 1604 five men met at the back of a shop near the Strand in London. Their names were Robert Catesby, Thomas Percy, Thomas Winter, John Wright, and Guy Fawkes. These men had two things in common. They were

all Roman Catholics and they all hated James I. This meeting was the beginning of one of the most famous conspiracies in history, the Gunpowder Plot.

Although Guy Fawkes is now the best known of the plotters, their leader was a wealthy landowner named Robert Catesby. It was Catesby who thought of the "Gunpowder Plot". After he had sworn the others to secrecy he explained his plan to them. A tunnel was to be dug under the Houses of Parliament and gunpowder smuggled in. Then when the King and his chief ministers were meeting the whole building could be destroyed. In the panic that would follow the King's young daughter, Princess Elizabeth, was to be kidnapped. Later she would be crowned Queen but her leading politicians were to be Catholics.

As the plotters listened they became more and more enthusiastic. None of them seemed to consider one very important fact. The ordinary people of England did not want the Catholic Church back again.

85

The plotters did not meet again until October. By then a few more Catholics had joined them. After much thought they decided to rent a house next door to the Houses of Parliament. From the cellar of this house they would be able to dig a tunnel underneath the room where Parliament met.

For two weeks they dug through the earth. The roof of the tunnel was supported by wooden props. At night they buried the waste soil in the garden or dropped it into the river. They worked hard and at the end of the second week they had reached the foundations of the House of Lords. Then came the most difficult part of all. They had to excavate through a wall which was almost three metres thick. For weeks they struggled. As they chipped at the solid stone it seemed as if their plan was hopeless.

One morning in January 1605 the plotters heard a strange
rumbling above their heads. They crouched against the wall
of the tunnel, listening fearfully. It was as if a search was
being made for them. Then they remembered that above
their heads was a coal merchant's cellar. What they could
hear was the echo of moving coal.

At that point they had a wonderful piece of luck. The
coal merchant was leaving and his cellar was vacant. As soon
as possible one of the conspirators rented it. There was no
longer any need for them to dig their tunnel. The coal cellar
led directly under the House of Lords.

The gunpowder had now to be brought to the cellar without anyone seeing what was happening. On dark nights the barrels of powder were loaded into a boat. Silently the plotters rowed across the water, their eyes peering into the darkness. No one saw them and eventually they had 36 barrels of gunpowder stored in the cellar.

Guy Fawkes was the conspirator chosen to light the powder. Fawkes was a brave man who had fought for some years as a soldier in Europe. He planned to use a trail of powder and a slow-burning match. Fawkes calculated that when the match was lit he would have fifteen minutes to get safely away. A boat would be waiting for him. Once across the River Thames he intended to go to Europe to get help from other Catholic countries.

By October 1605 the plotters were ready to strike. Now they had to wait, for Parliament did not meet until November 5th. Some of the plotters began to worry. They knew that there were a few Catholic lords in Parliament who would be blown up with the King. It was decided to send letters warning them not to attend Parliament on November 5th. Among those who received these warnings was a leading Catholic nobleman named Lord Monteagle.

Lord Monteagle was dining with some friends one evening when his servant came in with a letter. Although he was annoyed at the interruption Monteagle began to read the note. He stopped with amazement at the words, "I say that they shall receive a terrible blow this Parliament, and yet shall not see who hurts them".

Lord Monteagle's hand was shaking when he had finished. He made no attempt to keep the warning secret. After his friends had all read the letter it was decided to inform King James. When the King heard of this strange warning a search was ordered of the Houses of Parliament. Even then there was no alarm. Many politicians thought the letter was a hoax.

On Monday, November 4th, parties of soldiers began to search the Houses of Parliament. As they approached the plotters' cellar they saw Guy Fawkes standing by the door. He made no attempt to escape but calmly told them that he was guarding his master's fuel. At first they believed him and did not enter the cellar. It was not until some time later that they decided to question him again. This time he was searched and in his clothes they found a slow match and a tinder box. Immediately they pushed their way into the cellar and found the barrels of gunpowder hidden beneath piles of wood.

The officers dragged Fawkes to the King. When asked what the powder had been for he told them of the plot but he refused to reveal the names of the other conspirators. The King ordered that he should be taken to the Tower of London

and tortured. Inside the Tower Fawkes was put on the rack.
This was one of the most cruel tortures. It slowly stretched
the victim and dislocated every bone. For two days Guy
Fawkes suffered terrible agony until, at last, with his body
broken, he gave the names of the other plotters.

Fawkes's bravery had not been in vain. It had given the others time to escape from London. Catesby knew that their only hope was to persuade other wealthy Catholics to join the revolt. Scarcely stopping to rest their horses, the plotters rode north. The news of the plot followed them. Soon it was clear to Catesby that no one would protect them. As they rode desperately on the weather got worse. Throughout November 7th they struggled in vain to get help. At 10

o'clock at night, cold and completely worn out, they reached Holbeach House. This was the home of a Catholic supporter named Stephen Littleton. Here they were to make their last stand.

That night the conspirators stood around a roaring log fire trying to plan their next move. The powder for their pistols had been soaked by the rain. Foolishly they laid it to dry on the floor. A spark flew from the grate and three of the plotters were hurt by the explosion. To the others this seemed like a sign from God that the end was near. They could only wait and see what happened.

By next morning the Sheriff of Worcestershire, Sir Richard Walsh, had surrounded the house. The plotters refused to surrender and fired at their opponents. As the soldiers attacked Catesby and Percy stood back to back. Even as they raised their swords one musket shot killed them both. The others were either wounded and arrested in the house or killed as they tried to escape. Only Robert Winter managed to get away from the house. He was not caught until January 1606.

The plotters were taken to London and imprisoned in the Tower. They were tried for treason and sentenced to death. On January 30th some of them were dragged on hurdles towards St Paul's churchyard. The rest were executed the following day. Vast crowds came to watch their suffering. The people roared with delight as the conspirators were slowly and horribly executed. As for Guy Fawkes himself, he had been so cruelly tortured that they had to lift him on to the scaffold.

The plot failed and the conspirators paid the penalty. Then the government took revenge on every Catholic, although most of them had known nothing of the plot and very few had supported it. Catholics were forbidden to live in London. They could not leave their own districts without permission. They were not allowed to become lawyers or doctors. They were compelled to take communion in Protestant churches.

The action of a few men caused many innocent Catholics to suffer.

QUESTIONS

1. a. Why were Catholics harshly treated during Queen Elizabeth's reign?
   b. Which King succeeded Queen Elizabeth?
   c. Who was the leader of the conspirators?
   d. What was his plan?
   e. After they had begun to dig the tunnel why did it seem that the plan would fail?
   f. Why did the conspirators rent the coal merchant's cellar?
   g. How many barrels of gunpowder were stored in the cellar?

WRIGHT

WINTER

PERCY

h. How did Guy Fawkes plan to blow up the Houses of Parliament and then escape?

i. Why was Lord Monteagle told of the plan?

j. How do we know that Guy Fawkes was a brave man?

k. Where did the conspirators make their last stand?

l. When and where were the plotters executed?

2. In what ways did many innocent Catholics suffer after the plot had failed?

3. Act a little play showing what happened at Holbeach House. It can be divided into three scenes.

    Scene I.   Their arrival.

    Scene II.   The gunpowder exploding.

    Scene III. The fight and the capture of the plotters.

4. Discuss with your teacher when the idea of having bonfires and fireworks began.

5. Many people think that fireworks are dangerous and that "Guy Fawkes" celebrations should be banned. Do you agree? Discuss this.

GROUP WORK

Divide into groups and make a frieze showing the various stages of the plot.

CHAPTER 11

Sports and Pastimes

People in England during the 16th and 17th centuries played many of the sports which had been known in the Middle Ages. The poor played football, the wealthy hunted deer, and archery was popular with most people until the shotgun was invented. At the same time, however, new sports and pastimes were taking the place of some of the old ones.

Bear baiting was an old form of entertainment which became very popular in the 16th century. It was an extremely cruel sport. A special pit was prepared and the bear was chained to a stake. Then dogs were put into the pit to fight the bear. Powerful mastiffs or bulldogs were used for this. The bear had to fight off as many as six dogs at once. Often the dogs were killed, but there were always others ready to join in the fight. Bears were valuable and the dogs were rarely allowed to kill them. When the show ended the torn and bleeding creature was nursed back to health so that it would be ready to fight again.

Hare coursing or pursuing hares with greyhounds became a common sport during the reign of Henry VIII. Men walked through the fields about 180 metres in front of a pair of greyhounds. As soon as the men flushed a hare the greyhounds were released. Then the race began. The men watching gambled on which dog would win. Points were given to the dog which could turn the quickest and to the dog which killed the hare. In coursing the hares often escaped, for they have powerful back legs which enable them to go up hills very quickly.

Greyhound racing is still popular. Generally artificial hares which are worked by electricity are used.

When King James VI of Scotland became James I of England in 1603, many Scottish noblemen came to London with him. They had played golf in their own country and brought the game to England. The ball was made of leather stuffed with hair and feathers. The golfers used clubs which had different shaped heads. With these they could either hit the ball a long way or strike it high in the air when it was stuck in long grass. Although golf was played in Scotland it did not become popular in England for another 300 years. English nobles preferred tennis and the ordinary people played football.

Bowls became so popular in the 16th century that King Henry VIII tried to ban it. He said that it interfered with archery practice and bowmen were needed for the army. Despite this ban the game was still played.

There were two ways of playing bowls. The first was to play on grass with wooden balls. The balls were made with what is called a bias. This makes the ball turn either right or left and the game becomes much harder to play. The game of bowls which was played on lawns in the 16th century was like that played in parks today.

The other game was very much like ten-pin bowling. It was played in alleys at the back of inns, or in rich men's gardens. These alleys were sometimes strips of grass and sometimes wooden floors under cover.

Tennis was a very popular game with many wealthy noblemen. King Henry VIII became an expert at it. In the 16th century tennis was usually played on an indoor court. Although the racquets were strung they were heavy and clumsy to use. The rules differed from modern tennis. The object was to get the ball over the net and past the opponent, but it did not matter if it had struck a wall or ceiling first. In fact points were awarded to a player who could make the ball hit a wall and still go over the net. When played properly tennis was an extremely fast game just as it is today.

Celebrating May Day was an old custom which became very popular in Tudor times. The villagers went out into the woods on May Day Eve to collect flowers and branches. The maypole itself was brought in by teams of oxen. The villagers tried to make everything as gay and colourful as possible. Even the oxen had garlands of flowers hanging round their necks.

The pole was usually painted and erected on the village green. Then with everyone joining in, young and old danced around their maypole. They did not, however, dance with ribbons. This was not introduced until the 19th century.

May Day was a time to have as much fun as possible. Sports like wrestling, archery, and quarter-staff took place on the village green. Races were held and the villagers stood happily eating and drinking and cheering on the competitors. The merrymaking went on all day. The dancing did not stop until it was too dark to see.

Even today the May Day celebrations still continue in many parts of the country. Some village greens still have the stone base where the pole once stood. In others a young girl is chosen to be crowned as Queen of the May.

CHAPTER 12

The Pilgrim Fathers

JAMES I

One Sunday in 1608 a group of people gathered near to the village of Scrooby, Nottinghamshire, for their morning service. It was an unusual church in which they worshipped. Dressed in dark clothes, the men and women stood on opposite sides of the aisle. There were no ornaments on the walls. Nor was there an organ to accompany the singing. These people wanted their church to be as simple as possible. They were called Puritans, for they did not believe that the Church of England was as pure as God wished it to be.

At that time King James I was the King of England. He believed that everyone should belong to the Church of England. Despite this he had allowed most Puritans to worship as they wished. These Puritans at Scrooby made a great mistake. They said openly that everything about the Church of England was wrong. To King James I this was the same as saying that *he* was wrong. Although the worshippers in this picture did not know it, orders had already been given for their church to be closed.

The congregation sat listening to their preacher when the
church door was flung open. A party of soldiers burst in.
Their officer marched down the aisle. Angrily he ordered
the preacher to stop. As the Puritans looked up the officer
read out the King's order. The church at Scrooby was illegal,
no more services were to take place. In vain did the two
leaders, William Brewster and William Bradford, protest.
The officer would not listen. The King's command was to
be obeyed.

The closing of this little church was to be of great importance. Soon afterwards these Puritans fled from England
and escaped to Holland. The people who were later to be
known as the Pilgrim Fathers had left their homes for ever.

The Pilgrims lived for a number of years in Holland. Although the Dutch allowed them to worship as they wished, they still found it difficult to make a living. Also many of them wanted their children to be brought up as English men and women. They felt that they were becoming too much like the Dutch.

It was because of this that the Pilgrims made an agreement with a group of businessmen in England. These businessmen were prepared to pay for the Pilgrims to set up homes in America. In return the Pilgrims were to send to the merchants most of the food they grew and the furs they trapped for a number of years. It was a hard bargain, but the Pilgrims finally agreed to accept it.

In July 1620 forty-six men, women, and children sailed from Holland to Southampton in the *Speedwell*. At Southampton they met another party who were sailing in the *Mayflower*. Although these emigrants have always been called the Pilgrim Fathers, it is important to realize that the party waiting at Southampton were not Puritans. You have only to look at their clothes to see the difference. This party on the quayside at Southampton were not emigrating for religious reasons. Most of them were poor. They believed that in the New World life would be better for them.

At first these emigrants could not understand why the Pilgrims were so religious. Later, however, many of them also became Puritans.

The *Mayflower* and the *Speedwell* sailed from Southampton in August 1620. Some of the emigrants were only too pleased to leave England. Others gazed sadly towards the shore as they took their last glimpse of their country.

The voyage began badly. They had not been at sea long when the *Speedwell* was found to be leaking. The two boats had to dock at Plymouth. When the *Speedwell* was examined she was found to be completely unseaworthy. Nearly all the Pilgrims had to be crowded on to the *Mayflower*.

For almost nine weeks the tiny, overcrowded ship sailed across the Atlantic. The Pilgrims huddled below deck as the days slowly passed. Often they were cold, wet, and hungry. Even so they remained cheerful, for they believed that God was really on their side. As the ship sailed on, the Pilgrims planned how to govern their new land. Together they drew up what has been called the Mayflower Compact. They agreed that one person was not to govern them all the time. Instead they were to choose their own leaders each year. They also decided many of the laws which would be needed in the new colony.

At last land was sighted. As the ship drew near the shore
the Pilgrims stood on deck. Then together they thanked
God for their safe arrival. After weeks of misery they had
reached the New World.

They were soon to discover that it was not what they had
expected. The coast where they landed was cold and windy.
The soil was poor and full of stones. Dense forests reached
down to the sea. In the forests lived Indians who might at
any time prove to be hostile.

It was late in the year, and once the Pilgrims had brought their few possessions ashore they had to work quickly. With their professional soldier, Miles Standish, keeping guard against Indians, they began to build houses. At first these were only log huts with turf roofs, but anything had to do. It was too late to cultivate the soil. Instead each day some of the men fished in the sea. The fish caught were dried on the beach. The settlers knew that they would need all the food they could obtain in the months ahead.

The first winter was colder than anyone had expected. Icy winds pierced the frail huts. Deep snow lay in drifts around the settlement. In their cold, damp houses the Pilgrims struggled to survive. In this picture you can see how one family lived during that terrible winter. The father is making soup from cod fish and oatmeal. The mother and children crouch beneath a few ragged blankets. In the corner an old man lies dying. He was to be only one of many. For weeks every family was short of food. Rain and snow ran down the walls of their houses. One after another the Pilgrims began to die of scurvy and pneumonia. By spring, half of the party who had left Plymouth were dead. It if had not been for their faith in God many would have lost all hope.

At last the winter ended. In the warm days of spring those who were left could begin to improve their houses and till the soil. They were lucky enough to meet some friendly Indians. These Indians showed the Pilgrims how to trap beavers and also how to manure the land. They did this by putting dead fish into the ground where the corn was sown. That summer their harvest was good. By autumn they had warmer houses and furs to protect themselves. Food and fuel were carefully stored and when winter came the Pilgrims were prepared.

Although life was still very hard the Pilgrims slowly began
to prosper. In the years that followed the colony now known
as Massachusetts grew up. It was not long before other
colonists came from England to join the Pilgrims.

The Pilgrim Fathers had sailed in the *Mayflower* in 1620
because they wanted freedom to worship God as they wished.
When they had founded their colony they refused to allow
anyone else to have religious freedom. All newcomers had to
live exactly as they were told. It was because of this that many
moved away and started colonies of their own. These other
colonies have now become American States and include
Rhode Island, Connecticut, and New Hampshire.

The story of the Pilgrim Fathers is very important in the
history of America. They were the first emigrants to the part
of America now called New England. However, this is only
a small part of America and as you read other books you will
see that the people we now call Americans came from almost
every country.

QUESTIONS

1. a. Why were the people worshipping in the church near
      to Scrooby called Puritans?
   b. Why did James I order that church to be closed?
   c. To which country did the Puritans flee?
   d. What offer did the London businessmen make to the
      Pilgrims?
   e. What were the names of the boats which left Southamp-
      ton in August 1620?
   f. Which boat had to return to Plymouth and why?
   g. What was the Mayflower Compact?
   h. Who was Miles Standish?
   i. How did the Indians help the Pilgrim Fathers?
   j. Why did some settlers leave Massachusetts and form
      other colonies like Connecticut?

2. Imagine that you were one of the Pilgrim Fathers. Write
a diary in which you describe your experiences during the
first terrible winter.

3. Draw a picture of a Puritan man or woman showing clearly
how they dressed.

4. On a map of the world mark in:
   England; Holland; the route taken by the *Mayflower*; the
early colonies.

5. The Pilgrim Fathers emigrated for religious reasons.
Write a brief account showing why you would like to emigrate
and which country you would choose.

CHAPTER 13

Food and Cooking

This is a picture of a dining room in the house of a fairly well-off merchant in the middle of the 16th century. The floor was paved with stone flags. To make it more comfortable rushes were scattered about. The walls were plastered but over one of them was hung a large painted cloth.

There was very little furniture in the room. The one big table was a trestle type which could be taken down. The two carved chairs were for the father and mother. Every one else

sat on stools or benches. The only other piece of furniture was the oak chest beneath the window.

The table was covered with a table cloth. Some of the plates were made of thick pottery and others of pewter. Pewter is made from tin and lead. The family used spoons to eat with and they had knives with brass handles. At that time forks were rarely used, even by the wealthy. The light in the middle of the table was a rushlight. It was made of rushes soaked in grease, and burned very slowly.

A family like this would have had three meals a day. None of their meals seem very interesting to us. At about six or seven o'clock in the morning they had breakfast. This was usually bread with pickled herrings, cold meat, or cheese. Most of the family, including the children, drank ale at breakfast.

Their next meal was in the middle of the day. They began with soup or beef stew. This was followed by roast beef, mutton, or pork. They were also very fond of hot meat pies. Ale was again the main drink.

At five or six o'clock the family sat down to supper. This was rather like breakfast. It consisted of cold meats and bread and cheese. Sometimes they drank wine at supper time, but more often ale.

You will have noticed that the people of Tudor England were not fond of vegetables. In fact their only common vegetables were onions, and cabbage and peas which they made into soups. Potatoes were almost unknown in the 16th century.

For occasional treats a family like this would have fresh fruit, shell fish, or sweet pastries. The commonest fruits were pears and apples which were grown in orchards, and wild strawberries, raspberries, and blackberries. For rare surprises they had peaches or apricots which were grown in sheltered gardens.

This is a picture of the dining room in a wealthy person's house. Even here the floor was paved with stone flags, but instead of loose rushes it was covered with a plaited rush mat. The walls were panelled with light oak. At the back of the room a decorated carpet hung down from the ceiling to the floor. At night candles and rushlights were lit.

The table in the centre of the room was beautifully carved. Around it were a number of carved chairs. These often had cushions on them to add comfort. The sideboard held the valuable silver and sometimes gold plate.

The table was covered with an embroidered table cloth. The plates from which the people ate were made of silver. Look carefully at the drinking glasses. These must have been imported from Italy, for in the 16th century very few English-men could make glasses as beautiful as these. Even though this house belonged to a very rich person there are no forks on the table. The diners still ate much of the food with their fingers.

This is not a picture of an ordinary meal but of an impor-tant feast. The guests could choose from any of the food on the table. There was roast beef and leg of mutton, turkey, chicken, partridge, pheasant, and larks. Amongst the fish were salmon, sole, eels, pike, lobster, and shrimps. For those who were not hungry there were small slices of rabbit or chicken on toast. A large dish in the centre of the table contained a few vegetables like artichokes, cucumber, and peas.

When the main course was finished servants would bring in fruit tarts and sometimes raspberries or strawberries with cream. A dinner like this would last for two or three hours. As they ate the guests drank different wines which had been brought to England from Europe.

Next is the kitchen of a large house in the middle of the 17th century, about the year 1660. In many ways it differs little from the kitchen in the manor house which you read about in the book before this. There was still a bread oven in the wall. Much of the cooking was done over the large fireplace. Apart from the trestle table and cupboard there was very little furniture. The kitchen utensils which were not in use were usually hung from the walls. Most of the

utensils were made from iron or brass. The large jugs were
made from rough pottery.

As you can see the meat was still roasted on a spit, but if
you look up you will see that the spit is being turned by a
dog. On the wall was a round drum into which a small dog
was put. When the drum began to turn the dog could not
stop running. A chain connected the drum and the spit. It
must have been extremely tiring and unpleasant work for
the dog.

During the 17th century coal fires became more popular.
Coal was brought to London by sea from Newcastle. This
change over to coal fires was very important, for many parts
of England were becoming very short of wood.

   This is a picture of the dining room in the same house. Houses were still lit by rushlights or candles. The floor was made of oak and not of stone flags. People were beginning to put carpets on the floor instead of hanging them from the walls. The walls were panelled with wood. One of the most attractive parts of the room was the fireplace. This had figures of animals carved around the top. There was more furniture than in the Tudor dining room. As you can see it was very elaborately carved, particularly the table with its bulb-shaped legs. During the 17th century some very lovely silverware was made. This family had tea pots, a tea caddy, and candle-sticks all made from silver.

   Food did not change much from Tudor times. If you look closely, however, you will see that forks were now being used. Apart from the use of forks the most important change was that tea and coffee became popular drinks with people who could afford them. Not many could, for in the middle of the 17th century tea cost £3 10s (£3·50) a pound (500 grammes) and skilled men only earned about 2s 6d (12½p) a day. Even so it became a popular pastime for rich people to meet in the afternoon for what were called tea parties.

QUESTIONS

1. Which of the following foods were not eaten in 16th century England: chicken, pineapples, beef, potatoes, cucumber, chocolate?
2. In the chapter you saw a picture of a 17th century kitchen. This is a picture of a 16th century kitchen but on it there are six deliberate errors.
    Can you spot these errors?
3. Look carefully at the picture of a 17th century kitchen. How would you prepare a roast beef Sunday lunch in that kitchen? Why is it much easier to cook in a modern kitchen?
4. Try to visit a Tudor and Stuart house. Make notes of what you see in the dining rooms and compare your notes with these pictures.

CHAPTER 14

The Civil War

In August 1642, King Charles I, the King of England, watched as the royal flag was raised over Nottingham Castle. His face was sad, for he knew then that the Civil War had really begun. During the next three years the people of England were to be divided between those who supported the King and those who supported Parliament.

Today our Queen only helps Parliament to govern the country. In the 17th century the King had far more power than Parliament. Also he believed that God had given him the right to rule and no one should interfere. Many members of the House of Commons thought that this was wrong. They believed that the time had come when Parliament ought to be more important than the King. This was one reason for the quarrel.

The King also quarrelled with Parliament over money. It was the Members of Parliament who decided how much money Charles should have to govern the country. They never gave him enough because they objected to the way in which he governed. He tried to increase taxes and this made enemies of many wealthy merchants.

To make matters worse the King disagreed with many members of Parliament about religion. Charles supported the Church of England but most members of the House of Commons were Puritans.

The quarrel between the King and Parliament had lasted for years. At last in 1642 fighting broke out between them.

CHARLES 1

Both sides had to gather as many soldiers as possible. In this picture a royalist officer is trying to persuade the men of a country village to fight for the King.

The King got most of his troops from the North, the West, Wales and Cornwall. Parliament was more popular with Londoners, and with men from the South and East. Most of the lords supported the King, although some did fight for Parliament. However, Parliament had the help of many wealthy merchants. The ordinary villagers usually fought on the same side as the squire who owned their land.

The Royal Navy supported Parliament. This was very important, for it meant that other countries in Europe could not send help to Charles.

MUSKETEER   PIKEMAN

These are pictures of the kind of soldiers who fought in the Civil War. There were no uniforms at first and it was not always easy to tell friend from foe. Sometimes the two armies wore different coloured sashes over their clothes.

Right is a picture of a pikeman. Pikemen usually wore helmets and their chests were protected with iron armour. At their sides they carried a small sword. Their main weapon was the long pike. This could be nearly 5 metres long. The shaft was made of wood and the head of sharpened iron. Only strong men could hold a weapon like this. Even they had to press it firmly against their feet.

Also pictured is a musketeer. Musketeers wore no armour but they sometimes carried a sword. As you can see, their guns were very clumsy and had to be supported on a stand. The barrel was a metre long. Gunpowder and little round lead bullets were rammed into the barrel. At the side of the gun was a pan which was filled with powder. A slow match was pulled down by the trigger. The powder was lit and the gun fired.

CAVALIER

The cavalry was the most important part of the army. The King's soldiers have often been called Cavaliers. This was because Charles had the best cavalry at the beginning of the war. Parliament's soldiers were called Roundheads because some of them refused to have long hair like the Cavaliers.

As you can see the cavalry wore helmets and had armour to protect their chests and backs. They carried pistols and swords. The pistols could only fire one bullet. Then the horsemen drew their swords and charged down on the enemy.

During September and October 1642, the two sides gathered their armies. A few small battles were fought, but it was on October 23rd that the first important battle took place. This was at Edgehill in Warwickshire.

The two armies were drawn up against each other, waiting for the order to attack. At the word of command they advanced, and in the centre of the field a fierce battle was fought between the infantrymen. Man after man was killed but neither side seemed to be winning. Suddenly the King's cavalry charged. They were commanded by Prince Rupert, the King's 23-year-old nephew. Although he was only young,

RUPERT

Rupert was a fine cavalry officer. Bravely he led his men into the attack. The Roundhead cavalry had no chance against the King's Cavaliers. They fled before the sweeping sword strokes of Rupert's men.

It seemed as if the King had won the battle, but Prince Rupert made one grave mistake. Instead of attacking Parliament's infantry he chased after their cavalry. By the time he returned it was too late. Neither side had really won.

Edgehill was a drawn battle, but standing watching the two armies was a man named Oliver Cromwell. He was to become the greatest soldier of the Civil War.

As he stood there that day Cromwell realized one very important thing. Parliament would never defeat the King until their men were properly trained.

After the battle of Edgehill, King Charles marched his army towards London. The royal troops reached Windsor on November 9th. On November 12th Rupert rode ahead and stormed Brentford. The King's generals were confident that they could take the capital.

The people of London supported Parliament. Almost every man was prepared to fight against the King. They marched out of the city carrying whatever weapons they

CROMWELL

could find. When Charles rode towards Turnham Green he found an army of 24,000 Londoners opposing him. Even the wild Prince Rupert knew that they had no chance of defeating so many. Charles retreated towards Oxford. That town became his headquarters for the next three years.

During the years that followed the people of England grew used to seeing troops of soldiers. The Civil War caused suffering to many people. The armies, particularly the King's army, were hated because of the way they plundered the countryside.

This picture shows a lonely farm being raided by a band of Cavaliers. When this happened the harvest was taken and the farm animals killed. Sometimes the farm buildings were destroyed and the farmers shot.

It was on July 2nd, 1644, that the second really important battle took place. This time it was at Marston Moor in Yorkshire. Prince Rupert had ridden from Lancashire to relieve the town of York, which was besieged by the Roundheads. At Marston Moor he found himself facing a larger army than his own.

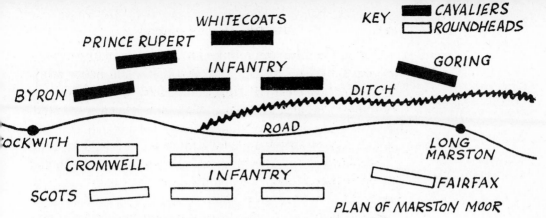

KEY
CAVALIERS
ROUNDHEADS

WHITECOATS

PRINCE RUPERT

INFANTRY

GORING

BYRON

DITCH

OCKWITH

ROAD

LONG MARSTON

CROMWELL

INFANTRY

SCOTS

FAIRFAX

PLAN OF MARSTON MOOR

By the early afternoon the two armies were ready to fight. Rupert waited but Oliver Cromwell had another plan. Evening drew on and Rupert and his generals thought that there would be no battle that day. Carelessly they left the field. At that moment Cromwell attacked. Hurriedly Rupert had to return to the fight. The Roundheads were ready for him. This is a plan of the battle. Look at it carefully and you will see how the two armies fought.

General Fairfax commanded the soldiers on Parliament's right wing. He led them against the Cavaliers who were commanded by Lord Goring. However, Goring's men fought back bravely and began to defeat the Roundheads.

On the left wing Cromwell led his cavalry against Lord Byron's men. Prince Rupert charged down on the Roundheads but then the Scots came into the battle. Oliver Cromwell had more men than Rupert and the Prince was driven back. Once Prince Rupert was defeated Cromwell led his men round the back of the Cavaliers and attacked Goring from the rear. It was this clever move by Cromwell that helped to win the battle.

In the centre of the field were the Duke of Newcastle's famous Whitecoats. These brave infantrymen fought to the end. Almost every one of them died for the King. When night fell the Roundheads had won the battle of Marston Moor.

Although he had reason to be proud of this victory Cromwell was far from satisfied. He knew that a still better army was needed to defeat the King completely.

Cromwell began to train one of the finest armies England has ever had, the New Model Army. He insisted that his soldiers were paid regularly. The infantry received 8d (3p) a day and the cavalry 2 shillings (10p). Out of this they had to provide their own food and uniforms.

Discipline in this army was very strict. The soldiers were well drilled and trained to fight according to orders. Any soldier who disobeyed an order was whipped. There were fines for swearing and the men were expected to sing psalms round their camp fires at night.

This picture shows a troop of them being led into battle. It was with this army that Parliament finally defeated the King on June 14th, 1645, at the battle of Naseby. This was the battle that really ended the Civil War.

Although the war lasted for a few more months there were no more important battles. King Charles fled to Scotland but the Scots gave him up to Parliament. He was put under arrest but was not kept in prison.

Even then the King could possibly have made a lasting peace with Parliament. Foolishly he refused to accept defeat. He supported a second civil war which failed hopelessly. After that Cromwell decided that the King was to be tried as a traitor to his country.

This is a picture of the courtroom. Surrounded by red-coated soldiers Charles faced the court bravely. From the beginning of the trial he said that Parliament had no right to try a King. He refused to plead guilty or not guilty. The days passed and Cromwell lost his patience. On January 27th, 1649, King Charles was found guilty of treason and sentenced to death.

On the morning of January 30th, Charles I was brought from prison to be executed outside Whitehall. It was a bitterly cold day. Charles wore two shirts so that he would not shiver. He did not want the people to think that he was afraid.

A vast crowd had gathered to see the death of the King. Soldiers stood guard in case there was trouble. The King had to wait all morning because the usual executioner refused to act. Even when another one was found he was heavily disguised so that no one would know who it was.

Slowly the King mounted the scaffold. He spoke a few words to the waiting crowd but hardly anyone heard what he said. Then the axe fell. King Charles I was dead.

For the next eleven years England had no King. During that time Oliver Cromwell ruled the country. It was not until 1660 that the dead king's son was brought back from France to be crowned King Charles II.

QUESTIONS

1. a. When did the Civil War break out?
   b. Why had the King and Parliament quarrelled?
   c. Who supported the King?
   d. Who supported Parliament?
   e. When the two armies did not wear uniforms how did they tell friend from foe?
   f. Which battle took place on October 23rd, 1642?
   g. What was the result of that battle?

    h. What happened at Turnham Green in November, 1642?

    i. Which side won the battle of Marston Moor?

    j. Which battle really ended the Civil War?

    k. Why did Charles I refuse to plead guilty or not guilty?

    l. When was Charles executed?

    m. Why did he wear two shirts at his execution?

    n. For how long did Cromwell rule England?

    o. Who became King in 1660?

2. Draw a picture of a pike. Indicate how long it was and how it was held.

    Draw a picture of a musket and explain how it was fired.

    Visit the school library. Look at a book on guns. Draw pictures of cannons and pistols used in the Civil War and explain how they were fired.

3. With your teacher's help mark on a map of England:

    a. The battle of Edgehill.

    b. The route taken by the King to Turnham Green.

    c. Oxford.

    d. The battle of Marston Moor.

    e. The battle of Naseby.

4. Write a few lines about Oliver Cromwell. Include:

    a. What he saw at Edgehill.

    b. Marston Moor.

    c. The New Model Army.

    d. The King's trial.

5. Discuss with your teacher what happened in your own district during the Civil War.

6. Discuss with your teacher the part the Queen plays in the government of the country today.

GROUP WORK

Collect pictures and drawings and make a book of the different types of armour worn up to the time of the Civil War.

CHAPTER 15

The Great Plague

This is a picture of a London street in 1665. The houses were close together and there were no drains. People threw their rubbish out of the windows, sometimes on the heads of those below. The garbage was raked into corners and left there for weeks. When the weather was hot the smell was awful.

The well-dressed man is holding herbs to his nose to hide the stench. His shoes are covered with the filth off the street. Flies bred in this filth and then carried germs to the food shops you can see.

It is not surprising that diseases spread, but in May, 1665, a terrible plague struck London.

By June, 1665, many people had begun to die. All London knew that the plague had come again. Purple swellings appeared on the bodies of the victims and nearly all of them died. Most of the doctors were ignorant and all sorts of medicines were tried. These are some of the treatments they used. Bread and butter mixed with treacle, vinegar mixed with rose water, and perhaps oddest of all, toads put inside the sick person's clothes.

When a plague victim died a red cross was painted on the door of his house. Over it were written the words "Lord have mercy on us". The door was then closed and no one was allowed out. Food was passed in by watchmen. The rest of the family had to wait inside the house to see if they too had the plague. Imagine the horror of being inside the house as you watched the remainder of your family die.

In the evenings carts came round the streets. The carters cried, "Bring out your dead". Then the dead bodies were collected. They were taken away and thrown into deep pits.

People realized that the filth in the streets helped to spread disease. As the plague grew worse many attempts were made to clean up the garbage. All stray dogs and cats had to be

141

killed. Unfortunately no one knew that it was a rat which really brought the plague.

Black rats were the true cause of the plague. They came to England on ships from countries like India where the plague was common. Lurking in the fur of the rats were fleas. It was these fleas which carried the disease. Almost any one who was bitten by one of these fleas caught the plague.

As the dirt was cleaned up the black rats found it harder to live, for they found their food in the garbage. Their real enemy, however, was another rat. This was the common brown rat. This rat, which you will all have seen, killed the black rat. Now comes another strange fact. The plague fleas could only live in the fur of black rats. As these rats died, so did the fleas.

Gradually the plague ended. It was believed to have killed over 90,000 people. Although it returned occasionally there was never to be such a terrible plague again.

Over two hundred years passed before doctors discovered the true cause of the plague. Now we take very careful steps to prevent black rats from getting into England. If you go to a docks you will see metal discs around all the mooring ropes. These prevent the rats crawling ashore. Also our streets are now clean and we know far more about medicine than we did in 1665.

QUESTIONS

1. a. Why was there so much rubbish in the street?
   b. Why was the wealthy man holding herbs to his nose?
   c. How did this rubbish help to cause disease?
   d. What treatment was given to people who had the plague?
   e. How could a person tell that he had the plague?
   f. What happened to the house of a sick man?
   g. What was done with the dead bodies?
   h. What was the real cause of the plague?
   i. What really got rid of this cause?
   j. What steps do we take to prevent the plague returning?

2. In your own words write a full description of a London street in 1665.

3. Discuss with your teacher and write down some of the ways in which we try to prevent outbreaks of disease today.

4. Although doctors were still ignorant, there was much scientific progress in this century. Discuss with your science teacher:
   a. Isaac Newton.
   b. The Royal Society.
   c. Harvey's discovery of blood circulation
   d. Halley's Comet.

SIR ISAAC NEWTON

DR. HARVEY

CHAPTER 16

The Fire of London

CHARLES II

In the 17th century most of the streets of London were very narrow. The upper storeys of the houses were so close to each other that it was possible for people to shake hands across the street. Many houses were made of wood and plaster. A few still had thatched roofs. At that time candles or rushlights were generally used for lighting. Sometimes these were left alight all night. Also in tiny workshops furnaces were often left burning. In such circumstances it was common for fires to break out and easy for them to spread. The people of London were used to seeing whole streets destroyed. However, on Sunday September 2nd, 1666, a fire began which was to burn down much of the city.

It started in a street called Pudding Lane near to London Bridge. Mr Farynor, a baker who lived there, was awakened at 2 o'clock in the morning by his servant hammering at the door and shouting "Fire!" Hurriedly the baker leaped out of bed. He dashed to wake his daughter and together they rushed towards the kitchen. To their horror they saw that the room was already a mass of flames.

It was too late to reach the outside door. Seizing his daughter's hand the baker pulled her up into the attic. Together they forced their way through the roof. Leaping down into the street below, they ran from house to house giving the alarm.

145

PEPYS

Although the mayor ignored the flames, others did not. Throughout the night and into the next morning attempts were made to fight the fire. Chains of men and women drew buckets of water from the River Thames. Almost useless fire engines squirted trickles of water. Fire hooks were used to drag the burning timbers from the roofs.

Despite all their efforts it was clear that the fire was winning. Even the Lord Mayor realized that the situation was grave, but he began to panic and no one would obey him. It was then that Samuel Pepys, the famous diarist, decided that King Charles II would have to be told.

Charles II and his brother, the Duke of York, immediately sailed down the Thames towards London Bridge. The river

and the streets were crowded with people struggling to leave the city. Furniture, mattresses, and cooking pots were loaded on to the carts which jammed the streets. Some people began to dig holes behind their houses in which to bury their valuables. Often they even buried wine and food under the ground in the hope that they would be saved from the flames. Cows, which were kept behind many houses, died in the fire. Birds flew helplessly over the roof tops until their wings were burned.

QUESTIONS

1. Explain why fires were common in London in the 17th century. Why did they spread so easily?
2. What different methods were used to fight fires?
3. A man named Samuel Pepys wrote a very famous diary in which he described the fire of London. This is an extract from his diary.
Sunday 8 a.m. "It being darkish, we saw the fire as one entire arch of fire about a mile long. The churches, houses, and all on fire and flaming."

Imagine that you were in London during the fire. Write a diary in which you describe the fire on three different days.
4. After the fire of London insurance companies became more common. They put metal badges on the walls of the buildings they had insured. These are some of these badges.

Discuss with your teacher:

a. How these companies organized these fire brigades.
b. Whether there are badges to be seen on buildings in your own district.
c. How people insure against fire today.

CHAPTER 17

The Massacre of Glencoe

In 1685 Charles II died. His brother James II succeeded him as King of England. Even before he was crowned many people did not want James as their ruler. They knew that he was a Roman Catholic, and most people in England were Protestants. Once he was King, James soon showed that he intended to make England into a Roman Catholic country again. A number of important politicians refused to allow this to happen. After much thought they decided that James could not be allowed to remain as King. His daughter Mary, who was a Protestant, was to be asked to take her father's place.

JAMES II

Mary was married to the ruler of Holland, William, Prince of Orange. Messengers were sent to Holland inviting Mary and her husband to become King and Queen of England. They were both opposed to England becoming Catholic

WILLIAM III

MARY

On December 29th Alasdair MacDonald set out over the moors towards the English fort of Inverlochy. He arrived next day and was taken by the sentry to see Colonel Hill, the commanding officer. The old chief explained that he had decided to sign the oath. MacDonald thought that the matter would end there. To the chief's dismay Colonel Hill told him that he could not accept his signature. Only the sheriff at Inveraray could do that.

When he heard this MacDonald realized his difficulty. Inveraray was 97 kilometres away over the mountains. He had less than two days in which to get there. As he opened the Colonel's office door he could see the snow falling on the hills.

The chief knew that he had to reach Inveraray. Wrapping his tartan plaid around himself he set out along the mountain path. It became bitterly cold and deep snow lay across the track. He did not arrive at Inveraray until January 2nd. By then he was already two days late. To make matters even worse the sheriff was not in the town. He would not be back until January 5th. This meant that when Alasdair MacDonald finally signed the oath he was five days too late.

The sheriff listened to the old man's explanation and promised to help him. The signed oath and a written reason for the delay were sent off to Edinburgh. When MacDonald returned to Glencoe he believed that his clan was safe. He had no idea of the tragedy that was to come.

The MacDonalds, like all Highlanders, were well known
for their friendliness. Although it meant sharing their food
with them they took the soldiers into their homes. This picture shows the inside of a Highlander's house. These houses
were made of stone with roofs of turf. There was only usually
one room. The windows were very small and covered with
skins to keep out the winter winds. This meant that it was
very dark inside the house. There were no chimneys and
the smoke escaped through a hole in the roof. The only
furniture was a rough table and a few stools. The floor was
made of earth and stones. The beds were of heather covered
with rough blankets and sheepskins.

They could not grow wheat on the wet mountainsides.
Instead they ate oatmeal. They also ate mutton and beef
from their own animals. Sometimes the men caught salmon
and trout in the mountain streams.

These Highlanders were very poor and their lives were
often hard and miserable. Despite this they divided what
little they had with the soldiers.

The days passed and the MacDonalds had no reason to fear that anything was wrong. On the evening of February 12th, Captain Campbell was playing cards with the chief's sons. Suddenly a messenger arrived from the fort at Inverlochy. The captain moved away to read the letter. It contained the orders he had expected. At five o'clock next morning every member of the clan under seventy years of age was to be killed.

Captain Campbell left the card table. The officers were called together. The ordinary soldiers were not told until later in the night. Many of them must have hated their orders. There is reason to believe that some of the clansmen further down the valley were warned by the soldiers, for they managed to escape.

At five o'clock next morning the signal was given. Two soldiers went into the chief's house. He rose from his bed to welcome them. Treacherously they drew their guns and brutally shot him. His wife fled across the room. They shot

QUESTIONS

1. a. Who became King of England in 1685?
   b. Why were William and Mary invited to become King and Queen of England?
   c. From which country did they come?
   d. Why did the government make the highland clans sign the oath of allegiance?
   e. Why did Alasdair MacDonald delay in signing the oath?
   f. Explain why Alasdair MacDonald was five days late when he finally signed the oath.
   g. What punishment was ordered for the MacDonalds of Glencoe?
   h. Which clan was chosen to carry out the order?
   i. On what day and at what time did the massacre take place?
   j. How many of the MacDonalds were killed?

GROUP WORK

Prepare a class book on the highlands of Scotland. The following are a list of suggestions. Drawings, pictures, and written accounts should be collected.

Scottish clan tartans.
Scottish dances and songs.
The "Black Houses" of the Highlands.
Scottish weapons.
Battles which took place in the Highlands.

CHAPTER 18

A Village Scene in Stuart England

Overleaf is pictured an English village in the 17th century. If you look carefully at the houses you will see many different styles of architecture. The very small houses had hardly changed since the Middle Ages. They were still made of wattle and daub and many roofs were thatched. Some of the larger houses were made of stone. They had attractive windows which jutted out into the street. The black and white house was half-timbered. It had a framework of great oak beams. At the end of the street were a few red brick houses. If you are observant you will see houses like most of these in many villages today. It is only the small wattle and daub houses which no longer exist. They were not well enough built to last for three hundred years.

Beyond the houses were the three great village fields. In the Middle Ages, as you read in Book 1, the villagers did not usually pay rent for their strips of land. Instead they worked on the lord's estate for two or three days a week. Long before the 17th century they had stopped doing this. Some of the villagers had bought their land from the lord, or, as he was called, the squire. The rest paid him money as rent for their land and cottages.

The farming methods had not changed very much. In many parts of England the villagers' lands were still divided up into strips. There were no fences except those round the hay field. The cows and sheep which grazed on the common land were only half as heavy as farm animals today. Some oxen were still used, but horses were much quicker at pulling ploughs and wagons. Seed was sown by hand. Scythes and sickles were still used to cut the wheat and hay.

The women outside the cottages are spinning wool. It was men who usually wove the cloth. They worked inside because the weaving looms were too clumsy to move about. When the cloth was woven it was carried away by packhorses like those in the picture.

168

The roads were extremely rough and it was almost impossible to use coaches. For this reason most goods were carried by packhorses. In this picture a group of men are working on the road. Each man had to work on the roads for three days a year without pay. The work was rarely well done. Usually the men just threw stones into the pot holes. These stones soon worked loose. In winter the mud was so thick and the holes so deep that very few people travelled.

Village churches are often very interesting places. Many churches were built soon after the Norman Conquest in 1066. As the centuries passed the churches were made bigger or parts of them altered. Look carefully at the church in the picture. The bottom of the tower was built in Norman times. We know this because of the shape of the door. The zig-zag pattern is also typical. Many Norman doors look like this. The rest of the tower is more elaborate. This was built in Tudor times in the 16th century. Usually it was the lord or a wealthy merchant who spent money improving the village church.

169

Sall